INDIAN RECIPES COOKBOOK

Simple Homemade Dal & Curry You Can Make at Home

(Healthy and Delicious Traditional Indian Dishes Made Easy)

Marna Christy

Published by Alex Howard

© **Marna Christy**

All Rights Reserved

Indian Recipes Cookbook: Simple Homemade Dal & Curry You Can Make at Home (Healthy and Delicious Traditional Indian Dishes Made Easy)

ISBN 978-1-77485-020-6

All rights reserved. No part of this guide may be reproduced in any form without permission in writing from the publisher except in the case of brief quotations embodied in critical articles or reviews.

Legal & Disclaimer

The information contained in this book is not designed to replace or take the place of any form of medicine or professional medical advice. The information in this book has been provided for educational and entertainment purposes only.

The information contained in this book has been compiled from sources deemed reliable, and it is accurate to the best of the Author's knowledge; however, the Author cannot guarantee its accuracy and validity and cannot be held liable for any errors or omissions. Changes are periodically made to this book. You must consult your doctor or get professional medical advice before using any of the suggested remedies, techniques, or information in this book.

Table of contents

Part 1 1
Channeh sabat 2
Palak rice 4
Sarson ka saag 5
Stuffed tomato 6
Indian vegetable curry 7
Turi bhaji 8
Chick pea - zuchinni curry 9
Serving size : 4 9
Capsicum masala curry 10
Chickpeas & potato curry 12
Chana masala 14
Mushroom pickle 15
Broad bean and cauliflower curry 16
Stuffed capsicum 18
Masala koki 19
Dhansak 20
Lauki ki sabzi 21
Mushroom pickle 22
Palakwali dal 24
Chole 26
Vegetable nilgiri korma 27
Chick pea curry 29
Carrot and tofu curry 31
Palak kofta 32

Tinday ki sabzi	34
Mushroom noodles	35
Spinach dal andra pradesh style	36
Chane ki tarkaari (curried chickpeas)	38
Shahi mushroom	40
Curried carrots & lentils	41
Palak paratha	42
Chili lima beans with fresh dill (dalna)	43
Palak bhajia	45
Methi matar malai	47
Masaledar nariyal lauki	49
Beancurd (tofu) in tomato sauce	51
Curried pineapple lentils	53
Chickpea and potato curry	54
Black beans in spicy tamarind sauce	56
Easy lentil soup	58
Karela masaledar	59
Khoya matar	61
Mushroom malai	63
Mushroom curry recipe	64
Palak tofu	65
Mushroom tikka	67
Potato red cabbage tikki	69
One pot tandoori quinoa	70
Spinach and potato indian pakoras	72
Bhindi bhaji - simple and easy okra recipe.	73
Poha (flattened rice)	75

- Baghare baingan 76
- Harissa lentils and cauliflower 78
- Chickpea and coconut korma curry with pumpkin 79
- Indian spiced baked potato chip sticks 81
- Potato capsicum curry 83
- Rava khichadi recipe 84
- Indian-spiced chard with tofu 86
- Vegetable dum biryani 87
- Daal: indian spiced lentils 90
- Indian-spiced eggplant & cauliflower stew 91
- Dal makhan 92
- Crispy potato red lentil dal 94
- Paneer bhurji kati rolls 96
- Rice and lentil curry bowls with cilantro cashew sauce 98
- Gobhi matar a homemade preparartion of cauliflower and green peas 100
- Part 2 101
- Introduction 102
- Idli or Cooked Rice 103
- Khatta Dhokla Recipe or White Dhokla 105
- Kala Chana Sundal 107
- Sama ke Chawal ki Idli 109
- Desi Tawa Cheese Biscuits 111
- Besan Toast 113
- Hara Bhara Kabab 115
- Aloo Tikki or Potato Fries 117
- Methi Thepla 119

Sabudana Chiwda	121
Rice Pakora	123
Appam Without Yeast	125
Onion Rava Dosa	127
Bread Pakora with Stuffed Potato	129
Eggless Cucumber Cake or Tavsali	131
Matar Kachori	133
Brinjal Fries	135
Cauliflower Fries or Gobi Pakora	137
Pumpkin Flower Fries	139
Gobi ke Paratha or Cauliflower Tortillas	141
MAIN DISHES	143
Braised Okra (Bhindi Masala)	143
Coconut Cashew and Golden Raisin Poha	145
Savory Spiced Zucchini Lentil Cake (Handavo)	147
Khichadi (Lentil Rice Porridge)	149
Baingan Bartha (Spicy Roasted Eggplant)	151
Aaloo Palak Saag (Spiced Potatoes with Spinach)	153
Vegetable Biryani	155
DAL / CURRY	159
Dal Makhani (Kali Dal or Black Dal)	159
Basic Buttery Mung Dal (Yellow Dal)	161
Mushroom Tofu Vindaloo	163
Chana Masala (Garbanzo Bean Curry)	165
FLATBREADS / RICE	167
Naan (Tandoor Bread)	167
Tomato Rice	169

Gobi Parathas (Cauliflower Stuffed Parathas) 171
SIDES... 173
Raita (Cucumber Yogurt) 173
Kachumbar 174
Cilantro Chutney 176
SOUPS 178
Tomato Soup 178
DESSERTS 180
Saffron Shrikand with Cashew, Golden Raisin and Honey .. 180
Date Cashew Fudge (Kaju katli) 182
BEVERAGES 184
Fig Milk (Anjeer Doodh) 184
Masala Chai 185
Fresh Honey Ginger Lemonade 187
Salty Chaas 188
Mango Lassi 189

Part 1

Channeh sabat

Ingredients

1/2 lb. chickpeas

8 cloves garlic, crushed

2 dried red chili peppers

2 fresh green chili peppers

3 medium onions, finely chopped

2 oz. margarine or oil

Salt

1 teaspoon turmeric*

1 teaspoon paprika*

2 teaspoons fenugreek seed*

1 tablespoon cumin seed*

1 tablespoon coriander seed*

Pinch asafoetida*

2 tablespoons chopped fresh parsley

1 large tomato, peeled, seeded, and pureed

1 green pepper, minced

1 tablespoon lime juice

3 cardamom seeds

1 inch whole cinnamon

2 tablespoons fresh mint, minced

1 teaspoon garam masala

*all ground finely together

Directions

Rinse and soak chickpeas overnight. Drain and cook 2-3 hours in salted water with a clove of garlic and green chili peppers. Drain when tender, reserving liquid. Heat oil/margarine and fry onions until dark brown. Add 1/4 cup chickpea liquid and cook until dry. Crush and add red chili peppers and fry over medium heat 1 minute. Add mixture of ground spices. Stir over low heat 1/2 minute, then add chickpeas, stir, and cook 5-7 minutes. Moisten with reserved liquid, add 1 1/2 teaspoons salt, parsley, tomato, green pepper, remaining garlic soaked in lime juice, cardamoms, cinnamon, and mint. Bring to a boil, then cover and simmer 20 minutes. Uncover and add garam masala. Cover and place in 350-degree (f) oven 10 minutes.

Palak rice

Ingredients:
1/2 bunch (cut into small pieces) palak
a pod garlic
a small piece of ginger
1 chopped onion
1 tomato
a few sprigs of curry leaves
1 mashed potato
1 cup basamathi rice
salt to taste
1/2 tblsp garam masala powder (optional)

for seasoning
1 tblsp mustard
1/2 tblsp urud and channa dal
1/2 tblsp green chillies and red chillies (cut into pieces)

Directions

First wash and cut the palak into small pieces and keep aside.

Then cook the basmathi rice and set aside.

Now take a wok, pour some oil and when the oil is hot, add all the seasoning ingredients and fry till done.

Now add the onions, tomatoes and cut palak and nicely mix and close with a lid.

Let the whole thing cook very well.

When it is done, add garam masala powder if you want and saute for a minute.

Take it wok from fire and add the rice and mix it well.

Take a wok, pour some oil and put the mashed potatoes and roast it slightly and when done add the curry leaves and put into palak rice and mix well.

Serve with raita.

Sarson ka saag

Ingredients:
500gms mustard leaves
200gms spinach
200gms bathuwa
3 garlic cloves
1 inch ginger
2 green chilli
salt to taste
1 tbsp maize flour
1 pinch sugar
2 tbsp ghee
1 asafoetida
1 pinch onions
1 tsp chopped red chilli powder
1 pinch turmeric powder

Directions

Clean and wash sarson, spinach and bathuwa. Chop the leaves finely.

Chop ginger, garlic cloves and chillies.

Pressure cook the spinach, sarson, bathuwa with garlic, ginger and chillies. When cool, grind it to smooth paste.

Heat ghee in a vessel, add hing and onions. Fry until light brown. Add salt and turmeric powder. Mix well.

Add the ground saag and simmer the flame. Cook for few minutes.

Add the maize flour, red chilli powder, sugar and stir well.

Serve hot with paratha or makki ki roti.

Stuffed tomato

Ingredients:
5-6 medium size tomatoes / tamatar
100-150gms paneer grated or mashed
1 onion finely chopped
finely chopped coriander leaves
2 green chili (finely chopped)
salt, red chili powder to taste.
Gram masala to taste
1/2 tsp turmeric powder
1 tbsp grated cheese
1 tbsp oil

Directions

Wash the tomatoes and set dry.

Cut the top of tomato (tamatar) like a cap. Gently scoop out the centers . Keep aside the scooped portion and chop the cut tops .

Heat oil in a kadhai add chopped onions and green chilies till tender.

Now add the pulp and chopped tomato and fry for a minute and all dry masalas and fry for a minute more.

Add paneer ,mix well and cock for a minute.

Fill tomatoes with the mixture.

Top with grated cheese and chopped coriander.

Place tomatoes in a cooker container .put little butter and pressure cook for one whistle. (or you can also bake it in a hot oven at 200 degree c for 20 minutes.

Serve the stuffed paneer tomato hot.

Indian vegetable curry

Ingredients:
1/2 medium-sized (100g/4oz) aubergine (eggplant) cut into 2cm x 1cm/¾in x 1/2 in sticks
2 small carrots (100g/4oz), peeled and cut into 2cm x 1cm/¾in x 1/2 in sticks
100g/4oz/1 cup peas
100g/4oz/1 cup french beans, cut into 2.5cm/1in pieces
1 medium-sized potato (100g/4oz), peeled and cut into 2cm x 1cm/¾in x 1/2 in sticks
50g/2oz/ 1/2 cup freshly grated coconut
4 fresh hot green chillies
2 tbsp white poppy seeds
1 1/4 tsp salt
3 medium-sized tomatoes, roughly chopped
1 tbsp natural plain yogurt
1 tsp garam masala
2 tbsp chopped, fresh green coriander

Directions

Place the aubergine (eggplant), carrots, peas, french beans and potato in a medium-sized saucepan. Add 250ml/8fl oz/1 cup water. Bring to the boil. Cover, turn the heat to medium and cook for 4 minutes or until the vegeatbles are just tender.

Meanwhile put the coconut, chillies, poppy seeds and salt in the container of an electric blender. Add 150ml/5fl oz water and grind to a fine paste. Set aside.

When the vegetables are cooked, add the spice paste and another 150ml/5fl oz water. Stir and simmer gently for 5 minutes. Now add the tomatoes, the yogurt and the garam masala. Stir gently to mix well. Bring to the boil and simmer gently for 2-3 minutes. Turn into a serving dish and garnish the vegetable curry with the fresh coriander.

Turi bhaji

Ingredients:
800 gms turi (peeled and chopped)
2 onions (chopped)
2 tomatoes (chopped)
2 tsp red chilly powder
2 tsp coriander powder
1/2 tsp turmeric powder
2-3 green chillies (chopped)
salt to taste
oil

Directions

Heat oil in a pressure cooker and add chopped onionsand green chillies.Fry Till they turn golden brown.

Add chopped turi,turmeric powder and salt.Mix Well andcook for 2-3 minutes on low flame.

Now add chopped tomatoes and cook till they turn soft.

Pressure cook it till vegetable is cooked.

Mix well and serve hot.

Chick pea - zuchinni curry

Serving size : 4

Ingredients
8 oz pasta (preferably whole wheat spaghetti)

2 tb safflower oil

Sm onion, chopped (1/4 cup)

Clove garlic, minced

1 1/2 c sliced mushrooms (4 oz)

2 x med zucchini, sliced

Lg tomato, cubed

15 oz can chick peas, drained (1.5 c

6 oz can tomato paste (2/3 c)

2 ts curry powder, to taste

1 c water

1/4 ts black pepper

Directions
Garnish: scallion curls, opt. (slice green part very thin lengthwise. Drop into ice water. Curls will form in about 15 minutes)

Boil a large pot of water; cook pasta until al dente.

While pasta is cooking, heat oil in a saucepan. Add onion, garlic, mushrooms, and zucchini. Saute until zucchini is tender but not mushy.

Stir in remaining ingredients and cook over medium heat, covered, for about 8 minutes. When pasta is done, drain well. Spoon vegetables over pasta. Garnish with scallion curls.

Variations: - add 1-2 t finely minced gingerroot; saute with vegetables

Capsicum masala curry

Serves : 2
total time : 20 mins

Ingredients:
2 big capsicums (cut into lengthwise)
2 onions (grated)
2 tsp ginger garlic paste
2 green chilies (finely chopped)
2 tbsp tomato puree
1 tbsp sesame seeds
1/2 tbsp peanuts
1/2 tbsp coconut powder
1 tsp roasted coriander powder
1 tsp roasted cumin powder
1 tsp turmeric powder
1 tsp red chili powder
1 tsp garam masala
1/2 tsp mustard seeds
1 tsp fenugreek seeds
few curry leaves
1 tsp sugar
1 tsp fresh lemon juice
3 tbsp oil
salt to taste
1 tsp finely chopped coriander leaves

Directions

Dry roast peanuts, coriander, sesame seeds and dry coconut. Grind them into a fine paste and keep separate.

In a pan heat the oil and stir fry the capsicum pieces for 2 -3 minutes. The capsicum should not lose its crunch. Take out and keep separate.

Now in the remaining oil add mustard seeds, fenugreek seeds and curry leaves. When mustard seeds starts to splutter add grated onion, chopped green chilies and ginger garlic paste.

Saute for some time add turmeric powder, roasted cumin powder and red chili powder.

Fry the masala and then add peanut sesame paste. Saute it again with the continuous stirring until the oil separates from it.

Now add tomato puree, salt, and sugar. Cook for 5 minutes and then add garam masala and 1/2 cup of water. Cook till the gravy thicken.

Then add the lemon juice and the stir fried capsicum. Cook for another minute or two and then dish out.

Garnish it with the coriander leaves. Serve hot with chapatti.

Chickpeas & potato curry

To serve 5- 6 people for an informal lunch

Ingredients

1/2 lb large chickpeas

1 medium-sized potato - diced into 1/2 inch pieces

1 small onion -- cut into small pieces

2 medium sized ripe tomatoes - cut into small pieces

1/2 tsp mustard seeds

2 bay leaves

1/2 tsp black pepper

2 tsp coriander powder

2 medium jalapenos -- cut into small pieces

1 small piece ginger

Salt to taste

2 tblsp vegetable oil

10 cleaned and cut cilantro leaves

Directions

Wash the chickpeas under running tap water twice.
Then put them in a deep saucepan and fill it up with water.
Soak the chickpeas overnight, for around 8 hours so that they become tender.

There are two methods for cooking the chickpeas.
Method 1: transfer the chickpeas to a small vessal and add 4 cups of water.
Keep the vessal on medium-heat and bring to a boil.
Then reduce the heat to low, cover and cook until the chickpeas become tender.
This may take around 45 - 50 minutes.

Method 2: pressure cook the chick peas.
This will take less time as compared to the above method.

In a blender, grind tomatoes, black pepper, salt, coriander powder, jalapenos and ginger to a fine puree.

Keep a heavy saucepan on heat and add 2 tblsp vegetable oil.
When the oil starts smoking, add mustard seeds.
Keep a lid handy to cover the saucepan, since the mustard tends to sputter and pop.
Add bay leaves and fry for 1 minute.

Now, add the sliced onion and potato pieces.
Cover and cook for 10 minutes, until the potatoes become tender.
Add the cooked chickpeas and the blended mixture and stir thoroughly.
Increase the heat and bring to a boil.
Keep stirring and cook for about 12 - 15 minutes, until the curry becomes a little thick and syrupy.
Remove the curry from heat and if desired, add 4 - 5 drops of lemon juice
--- this will give a slight tang to the dish.

Garnish with cilantro leaves. Serve hot with chapatis or pooris.

Chana masala

Ingredients
2 t vegetable oil

1 medium onion, chopped

1 large clove of garlic, minced

1 t curry

1 t tomato paste (i used ketchup, how embarassing :)

15 oz can of chick peas drained, reserving 3 t liquid

1/2 t lemon juice

1/2 t salt

Fresh black pepper

Crushed red pepper, optional to taste

1 t margarine

Directions
Heat oil on medium high heat.
Fry onions until slightly browned.
Reduce heat to medium.
Add garlic, curry, and paste.
Stir and simmer about 2 minutes.
Add chick peas, liquid, lemon juice, salt, and black pepper.
Simmer 5-6 minutes, stirring occasionally.
Add red pepper to taste.
Add margarine, stirring through to melt it.
Stir and simmer for 5 minutes more or until peas are softened and dish is hot.

Serve over rice.

Mushroom pickle

Ingredients:
1/2 kg fresh mushroom
1/2 kg water chestnuts (singhade)
2 cup vinegar (sirka)
40 gm jaggery (gud)
2 tsp red chilly powder (lal mirch)
2 tsp spice blend (garam masala)
2 tsp cumin seeds (jeera)
2 tsp salt (namak)
2 tbsp mustard seeds (raai)
2 tbsp aniseed (saunf)
2 tsp fenugreek seeds (methiana)
a pinch asafoetida (hing)
a pinch ginger (adrak)
250 gm mustard oil

Directions

Boil and peel singhade.

Wash mushrooms and cut them.

Let mushroom and singhade dry.

Grind jeera, raai, saunf, methidana.

Make adrak paste.

Heat 4 tbsp oil in a pan and fry singhade in it till it becomes light brown. Take them out.

Now fry adrak and remove it from the flame.

Add all the spices in it.

Now mix mushroom and singhade well so that masala is mixed well.

After 2-3 hours mix gud in sirka and cook.

Let it cool and mix with aachar.

Store in a jar and then put extra oil.

Broad bean and cauliflower curry

Ingredients
2 garlic cloves, chopped
1 inch cube fresh ginger
1 fresh green chili, seeded and chopped
1 tbs. oil
1 onion, sliced
1 large potato, chopped
2 tbs. softened margarine (can use oil)
1 medium cauliflower, floreted
2-1/2 cups vegetable stock
2 tbs. creamed coconut
1-10 oz can broad beans, with liquor
Juice of 1/2 lemon
Fresh coriander or parsley
1 tsp. curry powder
Salt and pepper

Directions
Blend garlic, ginger, chili and oil in food processor until smooth.
In large saucepan fry onion and potato for 5 minutes.
Stir in spice paste and curry powder.
Cook 1 minute.

Add cauliflower and stir well.
Pour in stock.
Bring to a boil and mix in coconut, stirring until melted.
Season well then cover and simmer 10 minutes.
Add beans and liquor, cook uncovered 10 minutes.
Add lemon juice and salt/pepper to taste.
Garnish with herbs.

Stuffed capsicum

Ingredients:
5-6 capsicum (simlamirch)
2 boiled potatoes
2 tbsp boiled green peas
1 onion finely chopped
1/4th tsp turmeric powder
red chili powder to taste
1/4th tsp garam masala
1/4th tsp dry mango powder (amchur)
salt to taste
oil/ghee for frying

Directions

Wash the capsicum and boil them whole till they are tender (not too much), drain water and keep aside to cool.

Mash the boiled potatoes.

Now in a pan heat 2-tbsp oil/ghee and add chopped onion and fry till it turns golden brown.

Now add all spices, mashed potatoes and peas and fry for few moments.

With a sharp knife cut the stem of the capsicum and take out seeds from the top gently and add the stuffing in it.

Now take oil/ghee in a kadhai and fry the stuffed capsicums on all sides.

Garnish the bharawan capsicum with grated paneer, chopped coriander leaves and thinly sliced rings of tomato. Serve hot.

Masala koki

Ingredients:
2 cup wheatflour
1 onion (finely chopped)
1-2 green chillies (finely chopped)
2 tblsp coriander & mint leaves (finely chopped)
1/2 tsp red chilly powder
1/2 tsp cumin seeds
salt to taste
2 1/2 tblsp desi ghee
ghee or oil to roast the koki (roti)

Directions

Mix wheatflour,onions,green chillies,cumin seeds,salt,mint & coriander leaves, red chilly powder,2 1/2 tblsp desi ghee and knead a stiff dough by adding little water.

Make equal round portions out of this dough (about six)

Roll out each portion in a shape of roti or parantha and prick it with fork all over to cook it evenly.

Heat a tawa and grease it with some ghee.

Gently place a rolled out koki on it and roast it from both sides evenly by applying ghee.

Serve masala koki hot with curd or chutneys

Dhansak

Yield: 4 servings

Ingredients
1 c mixed legumes
3 c water
1 lb mixed vegetables
4 tb oil/margarine
1 sm onion, diced.
2 ea garlic cloves, chopped
1 ea green chili, chopped
1/2 ts turmeric
2 ts garam masala
Salt to taste
1 tb lemon juice
3 tb chopped cilantro

Directions
Wash legumes & soak for an hour.

Place water & legumes in a large pot & bring to a boil. Cut vegetables into bite sized pieces & add to the legumes. Cook for 10 minutes.

Heat oil/margarine in a separate pot & saute onion & garlic till golden. Stir in chili, turmeric & garam masala. Mix thouroughly.

Transfer legumes & vegetables into pot with oil/margarine mixture & stir well.

Add salt & cook for another 20 minutes until everything is tender.

Add lemon juice & cilantro & serve hot.

Lauki ki sabzi

Ingredients:
1 medium sized or 700 gms lauki
1 medium onion (chopped)
2 medium tomato (chopped)
1 tsp ginger garlic paste
1/2 tsp cumin seeds
1/2 tsp red chilly powder
1 tsp turmeric powder
1/2 tsp garam masala
salt to taste
2 tsp oil

Directions

Peel and cut the lauki in cubes. Soak them in water otherwise the lauki will get black.

Heat oil in a pressure cooker and cumin seeds. Let it splutter.

Add ginger garlic paste and onions and fry till golden brown.

Now add tomatoes and rest of the dry spices except salt. Mix well and cook till oil starts to separate.

Now add lauki and salt and stir fry for 2-3 minutes.

Close the lid and pressure cook for 4 whistles on medium flame. If using a pan then cook the sabzi in a covered pan till the gourd is soft. Stirring occasionally.

If you feel that the sabzi is watery then put it back on flame and cook till the vegetable is semi-dry.

Tastes delicious with chapatis and raita.

Mushroom pickle

Ingredients:
1/2 kg fresh mushroom
1/2 kg water chestnuts (singhade)
2 cup vinegar (sirka)
40 gm jaggery (gud)
2 tsp red chilly powder (lal mirch)
2 tsp spice blend (garam masala)
2 tsp cumin seeds (jeera)
2 tsp salt (namak)
2 tbsp mustard seeds (raai)
2 tbsp aniseed (saunf)
2 tsp fenugreek seeds (methiana)
a pinch asafoetida (hing)
a pinch ginger (adrak)
250 gm mustard oil

Directions

Boil and peel singhade.

Wash mushrooms and cut them.

Let mushroom and singhade dry.

Grind jeera, raai, saunf, methidana.

Make adrak paste.

Heat 4 tbsp oil in a pan and fry singhade in it till it becomes light brown. Take them out.

Now fry adrak and remove it from the flame.

Add all the spices in it.

Now mix mushroom and singhade well so that masala is mixed well.

After 2-3 hours mix gud in sirka and cook.

Let it cool and mix with aachar.

Store in a jar and then put extra oil.

Palakwali dal

Ingredients:
2 green chillies
red chillies whole
6 -8 garlic flakes
salt to taste
2 medium sized onions
2 tblsp oil
1 tsp cumin seeds
a pinch asafoetida
1 inch ginger
1 tsp turmeric powder
1 tsp lemon juice
3/4 cup green gram split
15 - 20 leaves spinach

Directions

Wash and boil moong dal with salt and turmeric powder in 5 cup of water.

Wash spinach leaves completely in cold running water.

Then roughly shred them.

Take off onions and cut them finely.

Wash green chillies, de-seed and cut them finely.

Take off and cut garlic, keep aside.

Heat up oil in a kadai.

Mix in asafoetida and cumin seeds.

When cumin seeds start to change colour, mix in cut onions, cut green chillies and broken red chillies.

Stir fry till onions are soft and translucent.

Mix in cut ginger and garlic, stir fry for 1/2 a minute.

Mix in the boiled dal.

Bring to a boil and mix in shredded spinach and lemon juice.

Simmer (boil slowly at low temperature) for 2 minutes and serve hot.

Chole

Ingredients
Garbanzo beans (or chick peas) 1 tin

Onion 1

Ginger 1 tsp.

Garlic 1 tsp.

Tomatoes 1/2 can

Cumin powder 1 tsp.

Coriander powder 1 tsp.

Chili powder 1 tsp.

Tamcom 1/2 tsp.

Garam masala 1 tsp.

Coriander leaves bunch

Directions
Saute onions, add garlic and ginger. Fry for about 5 min- utes.

Add tomatoes, and continue frying.

Add cumin, coriander and chili powders, and some salt.
Fry for another 5 minutes.

Add garbanzo beans (or chick peas), boil for a few mintues.

Add garam masala, let mixture simmer.

Separately, boil tamcon in water until it dissolves.
Add this to main mixture.

Remove from stove.
Serve garnished with coriander leaves and lemon slices.

Vegetable nilgiri korma

Ingredients:
1/4 cup coriander leaves (dhania patta) chopped
10-12 curry leaves
1 tblsp garam masala powder
1 potato (aloo)
1/2 cup green peas (matar) shelled
1/4 cauliflower (gobhi)
10 french beans
12 tblsp groundnut (moong fali) oil
2 medium onions
1 capsicum (shimla mirch)
salt (namak) to taste
1 carrots (gajjar)
2 tomatoes (tamatar)
for masala paste
1" ginger (adrak)
1 tsp cumin seed (jeera)
2 tblsp poppy seeds (khuskhus)
12 cloves (lavang) garlic
6 red chillies whole
1/2 cup coconut (narial) scraped
2 tblsp coriander seed
2 tblsp fennel (saunf) seed

Directions

Wash and cut all the vegetables into equal size pieces.

Cut the onion.

Wash and puree the tomatoes.

Heat up two tablespoon of oil and fry the paste ingredients till light brown, cool and grind to a paste with little water.

Wash and cut the coriander leaves.

Boil the potatoes, cauliflower and carrots till half done in salted water.

Remove and keep aside.

Heat up oil in pan and mix in the onion and fry till golden brown.

Wash and mix in the curry leaves and masala paste.

Fry till the oil separates.

Mix in the vegetables and continue stirring.

Pour out the tomato puree and bring to boil.

Mix in two cup water and simmer (boil slowly at low temperature) till the vegetables are cooked and the gravy is thick.

Sprinkle the garam masala, stir well.

Serve nilgiri kurma hot.

Chick pea curry

Ingredients

3 cloves garlic, minced

2 tsp fresh ginger, minced

1-2 onions

2 tsp veg oil

1 - 1/2 cups peeled, grated butternut squash

1 carrot, shredded

2 potatoes, peeled & cubed

2 cups water

4 cups cooked chick peas (i used 1 can)

1/4 cup rice

2 tsp curry powder

1/2 tsp ground coriander

1/8 tsp cayenne pepper

1/4 tsp salt (i used 1/2 tsp veg stock)

1 apple, peeled and chopped, 1/4 cup raisins

Directions

Saute garlic, ginger, onions in oil until tender, add curry powder, mix thoroughly.
Add squash, carrot and potatoes, rice.
Pour in water, veg stock and remaining spices & chick peas & raisins.
Simmer until veggies tender.
About 10 minutes before serving, mix in chopped apple.
This seems best served slightly above room temperature.

Per cup serving: 186 calories; protein 6g; fat 4g; carbohydrates 34g; cholesterol 0mg.

This recipe rocks!
The combination of winter squash and curry is definitely a winner.
Grated butternut squash cooks up tender and juicy without falling apart into puree.
Try using some of the patak's curry pastes instead of the dry spices.

Carrot and tofu curry

Ingredients

Carrots - 2 big peices

Tofu - 250gms

Turmeric powder - a pinch of the powder

Chilli or paprika powder - 1/4 of tea spoon

Lemon juice - 1/4 of tea spoon

Coriander (cilantro) to garnish

Salt to taste

Directions

Grate the carrots , grate the tofu and keep it aside in two seperate bowls.

Now heat the pan and add two tea spoon of oil to it. once the oil is hot carefully add the grated carrots to it. fry it for a while and then add the grated tofu. keep frying for abt a min add the salt paprika and turmerci powder to it . fry it till well and finish cooking.

Add lime juice and cilantro to garnish it.

Hope u enjoy this dish

Palak kofta

Serves : 2 -3
total time : 50 min

Ingredients:
For the koftas
1 cup palak leaves (washed and chopped)
1 cup mashed boiled potatoes
few cashewnuts chopped roughly
2 tblsp grated paneer
1 tblsp fresh corander leaves
1/2 tsp jeera powder
1-2 green chillies (chopped)
1 piece ginger (grated)
1 tblsp maida(flour)
salt to taste
oil for frying

for the gravy
2 bunch palak
2 onions (blanched and make a paste)
2 tomatoes (blanced and pureed)
2 tblsp cashewnut paste
1 tsp ginger garlic paste
1/2 tsp garam masala
1 tsp jeera or cumin seeds
1 tsp red chilly powder
2 tsp fenugreek leaves
2 tblsp butter
salt to taste
1/4 cup cream

Directions

Take all the ingredients needed for the koftas and mix them well. Make small round balls and roll them in some cornflour.Now Deep fry them on low heat till they are golden brown. Drain and keep aside.

Clean the spinach and boil the spinach in very little water and salt. Add a pinch of sugar to maintain the green color. Once boiled drain out the excess water and squeeze out water from the spinach and make a fine paste.

Heat butter in a wok or kadai.Add The jeera and when it begins to splutter add onion, ginger garlic paste and fry till golden brown.

Now add pureed tomatoes and cook till oil separates.

Add the palak puree and cashewnut paste and mix well.Now Add salt, red chilly powder,garam masala and cover cook for 3-4 minutes. Add 1/4 cup water and let it boil. Then add cream and crushed fenugreek leaves. Mix well.

Finally add the koftas in the gravy and let it simmer for another 2 minutes so that the koftas absorb the flovour of the gravy.

Dish out the koftas in a serving bowl.

Garnish it with some swirls of fresh beaten cream on the top.

Serve hot with chapatis or naan.

Note: 1 add the koftas in the curry only at the time of serving. So you can keep the curry ready and at the time of serving place the koftas and simmer for 2 -3 minutes and then serve.
2. If You have a stale bread you can replace the maida with 2 - 3 bread slice. Remove the sides and mash them with the kofta ingredients.

Tinday ki sabzi

Serves : 2
cooking time : 25 mins

Ingredients:
250 gms tinda (scraped)
1/2 tsp turmeric powder
1/2 tsp red chilly powder
1/2 tsp cumin seeds
1/2 tsp amchur powder
salt to taste
2 tsp oil
2 -3 big green chillies
1 tomato finely chopped
few sprigs green coriander

Directions

Chop the tindas into wedges of medium thickness.

Heat oil in a wok or kadai. Add cumin seeds and let them splutter.

Now add chopped tinda along with rest of the powdered spices except amchur. Mix well.

Cook covered on low flame. When half done add the tomatoes and the green chillies slit lengthwise and mix well. Stir occasionally.

When till tinda is done and add amchur powder. Mix well. Garnish with chopped corainder leaves

Serve hot.

Mushroom noodles

Ingredients:
1 tin mushroom
1 cup noodles
2 onion (pyaj)
10-11 garlic (lahsun) buds
1 cup cream
2 cheese cubes
3 tbsp butter
1 tsp carom seeds (ajwain)
salt to taste
1/2 tsp black pepper powder (kali mirch)

Directions:
Boil noodles in a container with salt.

When it softens, strain and wash with cold water.

Take out mushrooms and cut into thin slices.

Keep the juice separately.

Finely chop onions and garlic.

Heat butter in a pan.

Put boiled noodles in it along with a pinch salt and fry. Take it out and keep aside.

Now heat remaining butter in a pan and fry onions and garlic until it turns pink.

Then add mushrooms and carom seeds for 2 minutes.

Then add salt, black pepper powder, juice taken out from tin and cream.

Cook for sometime and then add noodles and grated cheese.

Fry for a minute and then remove it from the flame.

Serve it hot.

Spinach dal andra pradesh style

Serving size: 1

Ingredients

2/3c masoor dal (red lentils)

1/4ts turmeric

1/8ts asafetida

1 saute medium of choice [sks]

2 dried red chilies, chopped

1/2ts black mustard seeds

1/2ts cumin seeds

2/3c chopped red onion

8 cloves garlic, cut into_1/4"_slivers

6 green chilies, halved & seeded

1 lg tomato, cut into 16 wedges

2 c spinach, packed & trimmed

1 salt to taste

2 tb cilantro

1/8 ts nutmeg

Directions

Wash the dal. In a large non-stick saucepan add the dal, turmeric, asafetida, and 2 cups water. Bring to a boil, stirring often. Reducethe heat to low and simmer, partially covered for 20-25 minutes,until the dal is cooked to a thick puree. Stir occasionally toprevent sticking.

Remove from heat. Heat saute medium in a non-stick skillet or wok. Add dried red chilies and stir until they turn light brown. Add mustard seeds, stir until they crackle. Add cumin. Stir.

Add onions, saute until translucent, 1-2 minutes. Add garlic and green chilies and stir until onion turns light brown, 2-3 minutes. Add tomato, stir until the skin curls. Add dal and 1-1/2 cups water. Stir, boil and cook for 4-5 minutes until it is a medium soupy consistency. Add spinach, cook for 2 minutes, stirring. Add salt, sprinkle with cilantro and nutmeg.

Source: my father, an excellent cook, is from punjab. This is his mother's recipe for spinach. Very simple.

Chane ki tarkaari (curried chickpeas)

Ingredients

5 t. vegetable oil

2 medium-sized onions, peeled and minced

8 cloves garlic, peeled and minced

1 t. ground coriander

2 t. ground cumin

.25- .5 t. ground cayenne pepper

1 t. turmeric

6 t. finely chopped, skinned fresh, or canned red-ripe tomatoes

4.25 c. chickpeas, drained

2 t. ground roasted cumin seeds

1 t. ground amchoor

2 t. sweet paprika

1 t. garam masala

.5 t. sea salt (or to taste)

1 t. fresh lemon juice

1 fresh green chili, minced (use more or less to control spiciness) 2

T. very finely grated fresh ginger (a food processor works great on this)

Directions
1. Heat the oil in a wide pot over a medium flame.
When hot, put in the minced onions and garlic.
Stir fry until the mixture is a rich medium-brown shade.
Turn heat to medium-low and add the coriander and cumin (not the roasted cumin), cayenne, and turmeric.
Stir for a few seconds.

2. Put in tomatoes.
Stir and fry until tomatoes are well amalgamated with the spice mixture and lightly browned.

3. Add the drained chickpeas and 1 c. water.
Stir.
Add ground cumin, amchoor, paprika, garam masala, salt and lemon juice.
Stir again.
Cover, turn heat to low and simmer for 10 minutes.
Remove cover and add minced green chili and grated ginger.
Stir and cook, uncovered for another 30 seconds.

Note: oil can be reduced to 2 t.
It is possible to omit the amchoor and not affect the recipe.

Shahi mushroom

Ingredients:
200 gm mushroom
4 onion (pyaj)
7-8 tomato (tamatar)
1 piece ginger (adrak)
2 green chilly (hari mirch)
1/2 tsp salt namak
1/2 tsp red chilly powder (lal mirch)
1/2 tsp spice blend (garam masala)
1 tsp sugar
1 cup cream (malai)
1/2 cup cashew nut (kaju)
3 tbsp clarified butter (ghee)

Directions

Cut mushrooms into 2 pieces.

Finely chop all the other vegetables.

Heat ghee in a pan and fry onions until it turns pink.

Then fry ginger, green chilies and tomato.

When tomato soften remove it from the flame.

Grind it in a mixer.

Then cook in the pan and also add salt, red chilly powder, spice blend, sugar, cream and cashew nuts powder.

Cook for 2-3 minutes and then add mushroom.

Cook at low flame until mushroom softens.

Then remove it from the flame and serve hot.

Curried carrots & lentils

Ingredients

1/2 c dried red lentils

1-1/2 c water

3 carrots, peeled & cut into 2" pieces

1/2 c chopped onion

1/4 c golden raisins

1/2 tsp salt

3/4 tsp curry powder

1/2 tsp fennel seeds

Black pepper, to taste

Directions

(i'd normally dry-roast the curry & fennel ahead of time, but that would take away from the ease of the dish)

Combine lentils & 1/2 c water in a 2-qt microwave-safe casserole. Nuke at full power, covered, for 5 minutes. (if water foams and spills over, add 1-2 tb more water.) Stir in carrots & another 1/2 c water; cover, and nuke for 5 minutes.

Stir in 1/2 c water and all the remaining ingredients; cover, & nuke for 5 minutes. Serve. (intended for 650-700 watt microwave; cook longer if yours is less powerful.)

Palak paratha

Ingredients:
1 cup spinach
2 cup whole wheat flour
1/4 tsp chili powder
1 tsp cumin seed (powder)
pinch of turmeric powder
1 tsp ajwain or carom seeds (roasted)
1 green chili
1/4 cup coriander leaves (finely chopped)
salt to taste
oil

Directions

Wash the palak leaves. Set aside 100 gms and cut it coarsely.

Blanch the rest and refresh in cold water.

Wash and de-seed the green chillies. Cut roughly.

Puree the blanched palak leaves and green chillies together.

Sieve the atta with salt and make a soft dough with palak puree, cut palak and water if needed.

Cover with a moist cloth and keep aside for 30 minutes.

Divide into 8 equal portions.

Roll out each, spread some ghee and fold into half.

Fold again into quarter and keep aside for 5 minutes. roll out into triangles with each side of 6" approximately.

Heat up a tawa and put the paratha over it. turn it and spread some ghee round it. turn again and spread some ghee on the other side too.

Fry till both sides are evenly cooked.

Serve hot with yogurt.

Chili lima beans with fresh dill (dalna)

Serving size: 6

Ingredients
1/4 c large dried lima beans
1/2 tb light vegetable oil
1/4 ts cumin seeds
1/2 c chopped onion
2 garlic cloves, peeled, -crushed
1 half-inch piece fresh -ginger, peeled
1/2 c peeled, chopped tomato
2 tb flaked coconut
2 tb chopped fresh cilantro
2 1/2 c water
1/4 ts cayenne pepper
1/2 ts paprika
1/2 ts salt, or to taste
1 tb chopped fresh dill

Directions
Rinse lima beans. Soak in water to cover for 6 hours, or overnight. Drain and rinse again. Set aside.

Heat oil in a small heavy skillet over medium-high heat. Add cumin, onion, garlic and ginger.

Stir and cook until onion starts to brown, about 4 minutes. Add tomato, coconut and cilantro, reduce heat and cook until tomato is soft.

Transfer to a blender, add 1/4 cup of the water and blend until smooth. (if necessary, add more water to facilitate blending.)

Combine beans, tomato-onion mixture and remaining water in a heavy 2 quart saucepan. Bring to a boil, reduce heat to medium, cover, and cook until beans are tender, but still hold their shape, about 1 hour.

Add cayenne, paprika and salt. Mix thoroughly. Garnish with fresh dill.

Per serving: 55 calories, 2 g protein, 7 g carbohydrate, 2 g fat (1 g saturated), 0 mg cholesterol, 181 mg sodium, 3 g fiber.

Palak bhajia

Ingredients:
6 - 8 tsp besan
1 tsp red chili powder
1 tsp roasted cumin seed powder
1 tsp ginger (grated)
2 cups spinach leaves, cleaned and chopped roughly
a pinch of turmeric powder
a pinch of asafetida
2 pinch baking soda
1 tblsp rice flour (optional)
salt to taste
1 tsp smoking hot oil
water for mixing
oil for deep frying

Directions

Take a big mixing bowl; add besan, red chili powder, cumin seed powder, grated ginger, turmeric powder, asafetida, baking soda, rice flour, salt and smoking hot oil. Adding rice flour and hot oil makes the pakodas crisp.

Mix all the ingredients well and add chopped spinach leaves. Mix well. Now add water little by little to make a thick consistency mixture.

Heat oil in a frying pan or kadai and then with the help of a spoon or wet fingers drop small balls of the mixture in the oil.

Deep fry in hot oil and turn them occasionally to fry evenly from all sides.
Note : do not fry the bhajias on high flame as the mixture will remain uncooked from inside. Also do not fry on very low flame as the bhaiyas will absorb excess oil.

Repeat with the remaining mixture to make more bhajias.

Drain on absorbent paper and serve immediately topped with chaat masala, chutney and sliced onions.

Methi matar malai

Serves : 2
cooking time : 30 mins

Ingredients:
200 gms fresh fenugreek (methi leaves)
1 cup boiled green peas
1 onion (finely chopped)
2 tsp ginger garlic paste
1 1/2 tsp green chili paste
1 1/2 tbsp oil
1/2 cup chopped tomato
1/2 tsp cumin seed
1/2 tsp dry mango powder
10 cashewnuts
1/2 cup fresh cream
1/2 tsp white pepper
1/2 cup milk
salt to taste

Directions
Take finely chopped fenugreek leaves in a big bowl and sprinkle 1/2 tsp salt on it. Mix well and keep aside for 10 minutes. Then squeeze out the water from leaves so that it loses its bitter taste. If you like you can even deep fry the chopped leaves and not boil. This will keep the leaves crunchy.

Soak the cashewnuts in warm water for 20 minutes and then grind in a very smooth paste using littel water.

Heat oil in a kadai, add cumin seeds when they start to splutter add onions and saute. The color of the onion should remain pink otherwise the color of the curry will become dark.

Add ginger garlic paste along with green chili paste and saute for 3-4 minute or till the raw smell stops coming.

Add the finely chopped tomatoes and cook till the tomatoes become mushy.

Add the chopped fenugreek leaves and cook for 5 minute. (do not cover the pan as fenugreek leaves losses its green color.)

As soon as fenugreek leaves has mixed well and nice aroma is emitted add the boiled peas along with dry mango powder and salt. Cook for another 5 minute.

Add the cream, cashewnut paste and milk. Let it simmer on the slow flame till we get the thick consistency gravy. Stir constantly otherwise the cashewnut paste may get burnt.

Delicious methi malai matar is ready to be served with roti or naan.

Masaledar nariyal lauki

Ingredients:
1" ginger (adrak)
3 tblsp onions chopped
1 cup coconut (narial) scraped
1" cinnamon (dalchini)
a pinch asafoetida (hing)
8-10 peppercorns (kali mirch)
2 tblsp oil
1 1/2 tblsp tamarind (imli) pulp
4 - 6 cloves
3 red chillies whole
1 tsp turmeric (haldi) powder
1 tsp mustard seeds (rai)
8 - 10 curry leaves
2 tblsp coriander seeds
1 tblsp cumin seeds (jeera)
1 medium size bottle gourd (lauki,doodhi)
salt (namak) to taste

Directions

Take off and wash lauki. Cut into 3/4 " cubes.

Dry roast coriander and cumin seeds.

Make a paste of roasted cumin seeds, coriander seeds, peeled ginger, garlic, whole red chillies, peppercorns, cloves, cinnamon, turmeric powder and scraped coconut. (reserve one tblsp of scraped coconut for garnish.). Keep the paste aside.

Heat up oil in a pan.

Mix in asafoetida and mustard seeds.

Once they begin to crackle, mix in curry leaves and cut onions.

Stir fry for two minutes and mix in lauki.

Stir fry for 5 minutes. mix in the masala and coconut paste, dissolved in 11/2 cup of water. Stir and bring it to a boil.

Dissolve tamarind pulp in water if it is too thick.

Mix in to the gravy. Add salt and mix well.

Serve hot decorated with grated coconut.

Beancurd (tofu) in tomato sauce

serves 4-6
preparation time 15 mins
cooking time 20 mins

Ingredients

Bean curd squares - 4

Medium size tomatoes - 5, diced into very small pieces

Garlic - 4 cloves, pounded

Medium size onion - 1 sliced

Ground red chilli paste - 1 tablespoon or as desired

Thick soy sauce - 1 teaspoon

Curry powder - 1 tablespoon

Garden peas - 3 tablespoon (optional)

Coriander leaves - as desired, to garnish

Oil - 2 tablspoon

Salt - 1/2 teaspoon

Directions
1) fry tofu square till golden brown; drain and dice into small cubes

2) heat oil in pan and add onion. Cook for 1 min or until soft.

3) add garlic and tomatoes and cook on medium heat for about 10 mins, or until tomatoes reach a pasty consistency.

4) add curry powder, chilli paste, soy sauce and salt. Cook for 5 mins.

5) add diced tofu and garden peas and mix well. Cook for 5mins.

6) remove from heat.

7) garnish with coriander leaves.

Best with plain rice, but good with breads and rotis like pratha, naan, batura and puri.

Bean curd squares would be available in oriental stores. Pre-fried bean curd is also available, but check expiry date on packing.
You may cook this dish without frying the bean curd if you so desire.

Curried pineapple lentils

Ingredients

Veg. oil

1 large onion, finely chopped

2-3 t. chopped ginger root

12 oz. split red (or other) lentils (the lentils turn yellow when cooked; yellow ones may turn beige!)

Approx. 6 c. veggie stock (or water)

4 tsp. curry powder

Large can crushed pineapple, with juice (i used 20 oz. can because that's what i had!)

Salt to taste

Directions
Heat the veg. oil in a pot. Add chopped onion; saute until soft but not brown, about 10 min.

Add the ginger; saute another couple of minutes. Add the curry powder and lentils, stirring well to mix. Add the pineapple and its juice. Add the stock (or water). Bring to boil; reduce heat; cover; simmer until most of the liquid is absorbed and the lentils are cooked to the nearly-mush stage (add more stock/water if needed). Add salt.

Serve over rice. For a whole meal, prepare a dry veg. curry (with potatoes, cauliflower and peas, for example) to accompany this dish.

Chickpea and potato curry

Ingredients

Vegetable oil, 4 tablespoons (or "as needed")

Black mustard seeds, 1/2 teaspoon

Cinnamon, 1 teaspoon

Cardamom, ground, 1/2 teaspoon

Cumin, ground, 1 1/2 teaspoon

Coriander, ground, 1 1/2 teaspoon

Fennel seeds, ground, 1/2 teaspoon

Turmeric, 1/2 teaspoon

Cayenne, 1/2 teaspoon

Salt, 1 teaspoon

Garlic, minced, 3 cloves

Ginger root, grated 2 teaspoons

Onion, chopped, 1 large

Chickpeas (garbanzos) 1 cup dry

Potatoes, cubed, 3 cups

Tomatoes, chopped, 2 medium

Water, 1 cup

Possible garnishes:
bananas, shredded coconut, toasted cashews, raisins, chutney, etc.

Serve with:
basmati rice (or other appropriate grain)

Directions

Soak the chickpeas overnight (or as you normally do). Chickpeas from a can are fine too, and quicker.

Heat the oil in a skillet (i start with a couple of tablespoons, then add a little more if it gets too dry along the way).
Add the mustard seeds and heat them until they start to pop.
* add the rest of the spices and cook on low for a couple of minutes.
Add the onions and saute until translucent.**

Add the potatoes and chickpeas, stir them, and cook a few more minutes.
Add the water, cover the pan, and simmer for about 20 minutes, stirring occasionally.

The potatoes should be tender but not completely cooked now.
Add the tomatoes, stir, and cover for another 10 or 15 minutes.

Serve with rice and garnish as desired.

Black beans in spicy tamarind sauce

Yield: 1 servings

Ingredients

2 c mexican black beans

2 cc tamarind pulp (see note)

1/3 c peanut oil

2 onions, chopped

2 tb grated fresh ginger

2 tb minced garlic

1 ts powdered hot red chile peppers

1 ts freshly ground cumin

1/2 ts turmeric

1 lg ripe tomato, finely chopped

2 ts ground roasted cumin seeds

1 ts garam masala

Salt to taste

1 c chopped cilantro leaves

Directions

Pick over and wash the beans. Soak them overnight in cold water to cover.

Soak the tamarind pulp in 2 cups hot water in a nonmetallic bowl for at least 1 hour.

Squeeze the pulp with fingers to extract as much juice as possible.

Strain, pressing the pulp. Discard the residue and reserve the strained juice and pulp.

Heat the oil in a heavy, shallow pan.
Add the onions and cook, stirring frequently, until they turn almost reddish brown, 10 to 12 minutes.
Add the ginger and garlic and cook for 5 minutes longer, stirring constantly and scraping the bottom of the pan.
Add the chile pepper, cumin and turmeric, and cook for 10 or 15 seconds.

Stir in the tomatoes and let them cook until they form a sauce and fat separates out.

Drain the beans and add to the pan along with 2 cups water. Cover and simmer until the beans are almost done.
Check the water level from time to time, and if the beans look dry, add small amounts of hot water.

When the beans have finished cooking, there should be plenty of sauce.
Stir in the tamarind, cover and simmer until the beans are very tender.
Stir in the roasted cumin seeds, garam masala, salt and 1/2 cup of the cilantro leaves.
Cover the pan and let rest for at least 10 minutes.
Reheat and serve garnished with remaining cilantro leaves.

Easy lentil soup

Ingredients
1 cup -yellow lentil(toor dhal in hindi)
1/2 cup onion,green peas,beans all finely cut
2 tspns ground garlic and ginger
1 chilly
A pinch turmeric
Salt to taste
A little vege oil
Coriander leaves for garnishing

Directions
1) clean lentils, soak for 10 min
2) in a pressure cooker/pan heat ghee, add cut onions and ginger garlic paste.saute for few min till good smell comes
3) add green chilly, turmeric and the vegetables,saute for 2 min till well coated with ghee mixture.
4) now add the soaked lentils and pour 3-4 cups of water depending on the thickness required.
5) close the lid and let the cooker give out 3-4 whistles in low flame.
6) remove lide, garnish with fresh corriander leaves.

This can be had alone or with garlic bread.

Karela masaledar

Ingredients:
2 tsp coriander powder
1 tsp red chilli powder
1 tsp turmeric powder
oil to fry
5 -6 bitter gourd
salt to taste
2 medium sized onions
1 tsp dry mango powder

Directions

Take off and reserve the scrapings of the karelas.

Give a slit on one side and take off all the seeds.

Cut karelas into thin slices.

Wash and rub two table spoons salt all over the karelas and its scrapings.

Set aside for 3-4 hours.

Wash completely again and squeeze dry the karelas.

Heat up oil in kadhai.

Deep fry the cut karelas till dark brown and crisp.

Take off the karelas and keep aside.

Slice onions.

Heat up 3 tblsp of oil in a kadai.

Mix in cut onions.

Stir fry for 3-4 minutes till they are transluscent.

Mix in scrappings of karela and let it stir fry till onions are a little brown.

Mix in turmeric powder, coriander powder, dry mango powder and red chilli powder.

Mix in the fried karelas to the above mixture and stir fry covered on low heat up for 5-6 minutes.

Mix in salt if needed.

Serve hot with chappatis.

Khoya matar

Ingredients:
1 cup green peas
500 gms milk solids (khoya) 500 gm
3 tblsp cashewnuts (broken)
1/2 cup bread croutons
1/2 tsp red chillies crushed
1 tsp red chilli powder
2 tblsp raisins
1/2 tsp turmeric powder
1/2 tblsp oil
2 green chillies chopped
1/2 tblsp ginger garlic paste
1 tsp sesame seeds roasted
salt to taste
1 tsp coriander powder
1/2 cup onion paste
1 tblsp coriander leaves chopped
1/2 cup tomato puree

Directions

Roast the khoya slightly.

Keep aside.

Boil green peas.

Heat up oil in a pan, mix in onion paste and stir fry till pink.

Mix in ginger-garlic paste and sauté.

Mix in tomato puree, turmeric powder, red chilli powder and roast till the oil leaves the masala.

Mix in boiled peas and stir.

Mix in salt, roasted khoya and stir.

Mix in broken cashewnuts and raisins.

Mix in coriander powder and stir to mix well.

Take off the heat.

Sprinkle cut green chillies, roasted sesame seeds, crushed red chillies on the bread croutons and mix well.

To serve assemble the khoya-peas masala in a dish and cover with bread crouton mixture.

Sprinkle with cut coriander.

Mushroom malai

Ingredients:
200 gm mushroom
2 onion (pyaj)
3 tomato (tamatar)
1 piece ginger (adrak)
1 green chilly (hari mirch)
1 cup cream
1 tbsp coriander leaves (dhania patti)
1/2 tsp salt (namak)
1/4 tsp turmeric powder (haldi)
1/4 tsp red chilly powder (lal mirch)
1/2 tsp spice blend (garam masala)
2 tbsp clarified butter (ghee)

Directions

Cut mushroom into slices.

Finely chop onions.

Grind ginger, green chilies and tomatoes.

Finely chop coriander leaves.

Heat ghee in a pan and fry onions until it turns pink.

Fry tomatoes in it and then put cream and mushroom.

Cook for 5 minutes and then add turmeric, red chilly powder, spice blend and salt.

Cook at low flame until mushroom softens. Then remove it from the flame.

Garnish with coriander and serve hot.

Mushroom curry recipe

Ingredients:
Mushrooms-250gm
onion-1 sliced
garlic-2 cloves
potato-1 cut into small cubes
mustard paste-2 tbsp
poppyseeds paste-1tbspn
green chillies
mustard oil

Directions

Cut the mushrooms into slices.

Add 1 tbspn mustard oil in a pan and fry these mushroom with some salt and turmeric powder.

Set them aside.Similarly Fry the sliced potatoes and keep aside.

Now add some mustard oil in the pan and when the oil is hot add garlic and fry till they are red.

Then add the sliced onions and fry then till golden brown then add some salt,turmeric powder and green chillies.

When the oil separates add the fried potatoes and mushrooms.Fry For a min and then add some water.When It comes to boil add the mustard and poppy seeds paste.

Cook them until the potatoes are done and before you turn the gas off add half a tspn of mustard oil.

Serve with rice or chapati.

Palak tofu

Serves: 2

Ingredients
3 cups spinach, fresh
½ cup raw cashews
½ cup hot water
½ cup coconut water
½ block / 6 oz firm tofu
2 teaspoons of canola oil
½ teaspoon kala namak
½ teaspoon curry powder
½ teaspoon paprika powder
½ teaspoon ginger powder
1 inch piece ginger root
¼ cup coconut milk
¼ cup tomato purée*
¾ teaspoon salt

Directions
Place the cashews in a bowl and pour ½ cup of hot water over them. Let them sit for about half an hour to soften them.
Pour the cashews along with the water in a blender and blend as smooth as possible.
Wash the spinach and add it into the blender along with the coconut water.
Blend again. You can blend until the spinach is completely fine, or you can leave some spinach pieces in there.
Cut the tofu in pieces.
Heat a large pan with 2 teaspoons of canola oil.
When hot, place the tofu in the pan and season with the kala namak, curry powder, paprika powder & ginger powder.
Pan-fry it for about 5 minutes.
Peel and mince the ginger root.

Add the ginger (minus a few pieces for topping later) in the pan along with the tofu.

After like 2-3 minutes, pour the spinach-sauce over the tofu.

Add in the coconut milk and tomato purée and a ¾ teaspoon of salt.

Let it cook for about 15-20 minutes and add more salt to taste.

Add thinly cut strips of ginger on top.

Mushroom tikka

Prep time: 30 mins
Cook time: 30 mins
Total time: 1 hour
Serves: 3-4

Ingredients (measuring cup used, 1 cup = 250 ml):
200-250 gms button mushrooms
½ tbsp ginger-garlic paste or crushed ginger-garlic (approx ½ inch ginger + 3-4 garlic crushed in a mortar & pestle)
½ tsp ajwain or carom seeds
¼ or ½ tsp organic red chili powder (1/2 tsp red chili powder made the tikka a bit hot)
¼ tsp garam masala powder
A pinch of turmeric powder/haldi
3-4 tbsp besan/gram flour
1 tbsp oil (to be used only if grilling or baking the mushrooms in the oven)
Salt + black salt as required or rock salt
Chaat masala to sprinkle
Few chopped coriander leaves for garnishing
Few drops of lemon juice as required and lemon wedges to be served
1 medium sized onion, sliced thinly with some salt & lemon juice added - served as an accompaniment.

How to make the recipe:
Rinse the mushrooms well in water. drain and wipe them dry. Trim the earthy base stalks a little. in a mixing bowl, take all the mushrooms.
Add all the spice powders, carom seeds, salt and oil. mix well. Keep aside to marinate for 20-25 minutes.
Preheat the oven to 200 degrees c.

After 20-25 mins, add the gram flour and mix well.

Bake in the oven for 25-30 minutes or till the mushrooms are cooked and tender and are browned.

After 15-20 minutes when grilling, you can turn the skewers so that there is uniform grilling.

If you want you can sprinkle or spray some oil on the mushrooms after 15-20 minutes.

Sprinkle some lemon juice, chaat masala, coriander leaves on the mushroom tikka.

Serve mushroom tikka hot or warm with a green chutney, rotis or naan or even bread.

Potato red cabbage tikki

Prep time: 2 minutes
Cooking time: 5 minutes servings: 4

Ingredients:
Potatoes, halved, boiled and peeled – 4
Red cabbage, finely shredded – 1 cup
Coriander seeds – 1/2 tsp
Cumin seeds – 1/2 tsp
Salt to taste
Onion, finely chopped – 1
Green chili, chopped -1
Garam masala powder – ¼ tsp
Red chili powder – 1 tsp
Dried mango powder (amchoor) – 1 tsp
Oil for shallow frying

Method:
Take a mixing bowl. Add all the ingredients to it except oil, and mash well.
Divide the mixture into 8-10 equal sized balls. Gently flatten them into a round shapes. Keep the mixture balls in a fridge for 1 hour minutes. (you can also roll these balls in breadcrumbs, if you wish)
Heat a flat pan on medium. Add some oil to it, and shallow fry the balls till they turn golden brown. Serve hot with your favorite ketchup or chutney. Enjoy

One pot tandoori quinoa

Yield: 4-5 servings
Cook time: 30 minutes

Ingredients
1 tb. olive oil
1 c. diced sweet potatoes (a small dice is best)
1/2 red onion, finely chopped
2 cloves garlic, minced
1 jalapeno or 2 indian green chiles, seeded and minced
1 tb. minced fresh ginger
2 tsp. to 2 tb. (i use 2 tb.; see notes) garam masala
(optional) 1/4 tsp. cayenne pepper
1 c. quinoa, rinsed
1 and 1/4 c. vegetable broth
1 and 1/2 c. cooked chickpeas (equal to one 15 oz. can)
About 1 and 1/2 c. diced tomatoes (equal to one 14 oz. can)
1 tsp. coconut sugar or brown sugar
Salt and pepper, to taste
Fresh lime juice (lemon also works), for serving
Chopped fresh cilantro, for serving

Instructions
In a large skillet, heat the olive oil over medium-high heat. Add the sweet potatoes and stir.
Cook the sweet potatoes, stirring frequently, for about 6-8 minutes or until softened significantly.
Add the onion and cook for another 2-3 minutes, stirring frequently, until softened. Add the garlic, chiles, and ginger, and cook for another minute until fragrant. Finally, stir in the garam masala and (optional) cayenne pepper and cook for 30 seconds.

Add the quinoa, vegetable broth, chickpeas, tomatoes, and sugar, and stir to combine. Bring the mixture to a boil, then reduce to a simmer and cover, stirring occasionally.

Cook until the quinoa and sweet potatoes are cooked through, about 20 minutes. If there seems to be too much liquid, simmer uncovered for a few minutes to evaporate the excess. If the liquid runs out before the quinoa is done, add more water or broth and continue simmering. Add salt, pepper, and additional garam masala and cayenne to taste.

Serve with a squeeze of fresh lime or lemon juice and a generous sprinkle of chopped cilantro.

Spinach and potato indian pakoras

Yield: 6 servings

Ingredients
2 cups besan, chick pea flour
1/2 teaspoon aluminum free baking powder
1/2 teaspoon garam masala
1/2 teaspoon coriander powder
1/2 teaspoon celtic salt
1/2 teaspoon chilli powder
1 cup warm water
3-4 medium potatoes, finely chopped
4-6 oz fresh spinach

Directions
In a large mixing bowl, mix together the besan, spices, salt, and baking powder.
Add the water and mix thoroughly. The batter should be thick, almost like heavy double cream and there should be air bubbles throughout (like in the picture).
Incorporate the chopped potatoes and spinach and mix.
On a heavy deep sauce pan heat any neutral oil of your choice , i use olive oil. Carefully place in heaping tablespoonfuls of batter into the hot oil.
Try not to overcrowd the oil because it will result in greasy pakoras. Fry until the pakoras are a pecan-brown, about 60-90 seconds on each side.
Drain on paper towels. Repeat with the remainder of the batter and serve.

Bhindi bhaji - simple and easy okra recipe.

Ingredients (measuring cup used, 1 cup = 250 ml):
250 gms bhindi or okra or lady finger
1 green chili, chopped
1 medium or large sized onion, chopped
1 large tomato, chopped
1 tsp fennel/saunf powder
1 tsp coriander powder (dhania)
½ tsp turmeric powder (haldi)
A pinch of asafoetida/hing
A pinch or two of dry mango powder/amchur powder
¼ tsp garam masala powder
2 tbsp oil
Salt as required
Few chopped coriander leaves for garnishing

How to make the recipe:
Rinse the bhindi (okra) well with water.
Dry each bhindi with kitchen napkin.
Remove the head and the tail and chop the bhindi into round pieces.
Heat oil in pan or wok.
Fry the onions till transparent.
Now add the green chili and tomatoes.
Saute them for a couple of minutes till the tomatoes become soft.
Add all the dry spice powders one by one.
Stir and then add bhindi/okra.
Mix well.
Add salt.
Place a lid with a rim on the pan or kadai.
Pour water on the lid.
Cook the bhindi till done on medium to low flame.

Keep on checking in between so that the bhindi bhaji or sabzi does not stick to the bottom of the pan.
When the bhindi is cooked, then garnish with chopped coriander leaves and serve bhindi bhaji hot.

Poha (flattened rice)

Ingredients
(makes ~3 cups)
2-3 cups (when dry) (thick) poha (flattened rice)
a pinch asafoetida
1 teaspoon mustard seeds
1-2 green chilies (chopped small) (or according to desired level of heat - can leave out if you prefer)
1 onion (small dice)
1 potato (small dice – use the waxy kind, i.e. red bliss, yukon gold, eastern white. Avoid boiling potatoes, which don't retain their shape once cooked)
1/2 cup peanuts or cashews
3/4 teaspoon turmeric
4-5 curry leaves
salt to taste
1/2 cup fresh cilantro (chopped) for garnish
fresh lemon (to squeeze at end)

Directions
soak the poha for 5 mins then drain in a colander (there's a thick and a thin poha - this recipe is for the thick poha). Heat oil in a pan (devesh uses a wok). Season with asafoetida, then mustard seeds. As soon as they crackle, add diced onion and green chilies. Fry until translucent.
In parallel, heat diced potatoes in microwave for ~2 minutes to partly cook them. Add turmeric and curry leaves to hot oil once onions are done. Add nuts. Add heated potatoes. Sauté until potatoes are done. Add poha and salt and mix thoroughly. Cook for 3-4 minutes.
Transfer to serving bowl and sprinkle with fresh chopped cilantro and lemon juice (or lime juice) before serving.

Baghare baingan

Serves: 2

Ingredients
6 baby eggplants
3 tablespoons oil
1 onion, small, chopped fine
1.25 teaspoons ginger-garlic paste
½ teaspoon mustard seeds
¼ teaspoon onion seeds [kalonji]
¼ teaspoon fennel seeds
5-6 curry leaves
2 green chili, chopped
¼ teaspoon cumin powder
½ teaspoon coriander powder
½ teaspoon paprika powder
¼ teaspoon red chili powder
¼ teaspoon turmeric powder
¼ teaspoon garam masala powder
1 teaspoon sugar
1 teaspoon tamarind pulp
Water
Salt, to taste
Coriander leaves, to garnish
To be roasted and grind to a fine paste
4 tablespoons peanuts
3 tablespoons coconut [use fresh for best result]
2 teaspoons sesame seeds [till]
1 teaspoon poppy seeds [khus khus]

Instructions
Make the paste

In a pan dry roast coconut, peanuts, sesame seeds and poppy seeds (khus khus).

Roast for 5-6 minutes till you get a nice aroma and then transfer to a blender.

Add little water [if required] and blend it to a fine paste. Set aside.

Curry

In a pan heat 2 tablespoons of oil on medium heat.

Add the eggplants and cook on medium heat till eggplants are little soft, around 10-12 minutes. Remember you don't want them to be too soft.

Remove the eggplants from pan and place on a kitchen towel. In the same pan add 1 tablespoon of oil on medium heat. Once the oil is hot add mustard seeds and let them crackle. Then add onion seeds and fennel seeds.

Add chopped green chilli and curry leaves and mix.

Add chopped onions and cook till they are translucent. Then add ginger-garlic paste and cook till the raw smell goes away, around 2-3 minutes.

Once the ginger-garlic is cooked, add the dry spices - cumin powder, coriander powder and red chilli powder. Also add the salt and mix.

Cook the spices for 2-3 minutes, add around ½ cup of water to make sure spices don't burn.

Now add the coconut-peanut paste to the pan.

Add turmeric powder and paprika powder and cook the paste for 5-6 minutes on medium-low flame.

Add the fried eggplants to the masala and mix.

Now add 2 cups of water, cover and cook the curry on medium-low flame for 15-20 minutes.

Add garam masala, tamarind pulp, sugar and mix.

Switch off the flame, add some fresh coriander leaves and serve immediately.

Harissa lentils and cauliflower

serves: 2-3

Ingredients
Harissa
2 clove garlic
1 roasted red bell pepper*
2 chipotle peppers in adobo sauce
3 tablespoons adobo sauce
1 teaspoon cumin powder
1/2 teaspoon sea salt
2 tablespoons olive oil
Juice from one lime
1/3 cup cilantro

Lentils
1 tablespoon olive oil
1/2 small red onion
2 cups small cauliflower florets
1/2 cup red lentils
1 cup stewed tomatoes
1-2 cups low-sodium vegetable broth

Instructions
In a blender or food processor, pulse garlic until minced. Add remaining ingredients and pulse until harissa is well combined. Taste and adjust seasoning as desired.
In a large skillet, heat olive oil over medium-low. Add onion and sauté until translucent, 6-7 minutes. Add cauliflower and continue to cook for another 5-6 minutes. Stir in lentils, stewed tomatoes, 3/4 cup of the harissa, and 1 cup vegetable broth. Bring to a boil, reduce to a simmer, cover, and let cook until lentils are tender, 20-24 minutes.
Serve over grains.

Chickpea and coconut korma curry with pumpkin

Total time-1hour
Serves: 6

Ingredients
2 cups (300g) pumpkin pieces
1 tablespoon olive oil
Salt and black pepper, to taste
1 tablespoon ghee or coconut oil
1 red onion, thinly sliced
3 garlic cloves, minced
2 tablespoons grated ginger
2 tablespoons chopped coriander root
1 teaspoon fennel seeds
½ teaspoon ground cardamom
1 teaspoon ground cinnamon
1 teaspoon garam masala
1 teaspoon ground cumin
1½ teaspoon sea salt flakes
½ teaspoon cayenne pepper
1 tablespoon raw sugar
400ml coconut milk
250ml veg stock
Handful of tuscan kale leaves, chopped
2 x 400g can chickpeas
Lime wedges, to serve
Slivered almonds, to serve
Fresh coriander leaves, to serve
Steamed rice, to serve

Instructions

Pre-heat oven to 180c. Line a baking sheet with baking paper. Place pumpkin pieces, olive oil, salt and pepper in a bowl. Toss to combine. Place pumpkin on prepared sheet and bake in pre-heated oven for approximately 15 minutes until pumpkin is just done. Remove from oven and set aside.

Heat ghee/coconut oil in a large cast-iron pan on high. Add the onion, garlic, ginger, coriander root and fennel seeds. Sauté for a couple of minutes until onion becomes soft.

Reduce heat to low. Add spices, salt and sugar. Cook for a few minutes, stirring constantly till the spices are cooked through. Add the coconut milk, veggie stock and chickpeas. Increase heat to medium and simmer for 20 minutes until curry turns a shade darker and becomes really fragrant.

Remove from heat. Stir through the kale leaves and roast pumpkin pieces. Top with slivered almonds, coriander leaves and serve with lime wedges over rice.

Indian spiced baked potato chip sticks

Serves about 2

Ingredients
1 large russet potato (about 10 oz)
1 tablespoon vegetable oil or ghee
¼ teaspoon ground turmeric
¼ teaspoon or to taste chili powder pr cayenne powder
10 curry leaves
1/2 teaspoon salt

Directions
Wash and dry the potato. Peel The potato if you like. I leave the skin on because i like the texture of potato skin in my chips.
Slice the potato into 1/8th inch thick slices lengthwise using a mandoline or a large, sharp knife. Stack up the slices, and cut them lengthwise to form thin sticks, about 1/4th the thickness of a french fry.
Place the potato sticks on a kitchen towel, and gently pat dry. In a bowl, whisk together the ghee or melted butter or oil, turmeric, chili powder, curry leaves and salt. Add the potato sticks to the bowl and toss well. Now follow one of the below methods.
Oven method – pre-heat oven to 400f. Place the seasoned potato sticks on a non-stick baking sheet or a regular baking sheet lined with parchment paper or silicone non-stick mat. Spread the potato sticks so that they are in a single layer and don't overlap. You may need to do this in batches. Make sure they are in a single layer, this is what makes them crisp! Bake for 10 minutes or till the chips are golden and crisp. Halfway through baking, check on the chips, and remove any pieces that are already crispy and golden. Rotate the baking sheet and continue baking.

Microwave method – take a microwaveable plate and coat with a few drops of oil. Place the potato chips that have been coated in the turmeric chili ghee/oil. Spead them out into a single layer. You may need to do this in batches. Microwave on high for 2-4 minutes or until the chips are golden and crisp. Cooking time will vary depending on the microwave, so check on the chips periodically

Potato capsicum curry

Total time-20 mins
Serves: 4

Ingredients:
Potato, medium – 3
Capsicum (bell pepper), medium – 1
Onion – 1
Red chili powder – 1 tsp
Turmeric powder – ¼ tsp
Mustard seeds – ½ tsp
Urad dal – 1 tsp
Kasuri methi (dried fenugreek leaves) – 1 tsp
Salt – to taste
Oil – 1 tbsp

Instructions:
Pressure cook potatoes in enough water for 2 whistles. Peel the skin off and either cube them or crumble with your hands into big pieces and keep aside.
Chop the onions finely. Cube capsicum and keep it ready.
Heat a pan/wok with oil. Add mustard seeds and when they splutter, add urad dal and roast for 1 sec.
Add onions and sauté till it turns translucent. Now add the capsicum and sauté for another minute till it softens.
Add cubed potatoes, turmeric powder, red chili powder, salt and mix well.
Cook over medium flame for 4-5 minutes, mixing in between till the raw smell of the spice powders go off and the vegetables get slightly roasted.
Crush the kasuri methi between your palm and sprinkle over the curry. Mix well and take off stove.
Serve hot with either rice or chapathis.

Rava khichadi recipe

Prep time: 5 mins
cook time: 15 mins
serves: 3

Ingredients:
Rava (semolina/suji) – 1 cup
Onion – 1
Carrot, small – 1
Potato, small – 1
Fresh peas – 1/4 cup
Ginger – 1 inch piece
Green chili – 3
Turmeric powder – 1/2 tsp
Mustard seeds – 1 tsp
Cloves – 2
Cardamom – 1
Cinnamon stick – 1 inch piece
Bay leaf – 1
Cashew nuts, halved – 10
Curry leaf – 1 sprig
Water – 3 cups
Salt – to taste
Ghee (clarified butter) – 1 tbsp (optional)
Oil – 2 tbsp

Instructions:
Chop the onions finely. Thinly slice the potatoes and carrots. Microwave carrots, potatoes, green peas at high for 2 minutes. You can also blanch them. Keep aside.
Grind both green chili and ginger without adding any water and keep aside.

Heat ghee in a pan, add the cashews and roast till golden brown, drain and keep aside.

Add oil to the same pan. Add cloves, cardamom, cinnamon and bay leaf and sauté till you get the aroma.

Add mustard seeds and let them crackle. Now add onions, curry leaves and sauté till the onions turn pink.

Add the ground ginger and chili paste, mix well and cook for a minute.

Add rava, turmeric powder, salt and keep sautéing over low flame for 2-3 minutes. The rava will get roasted well.

Raise the flame to full. Add the blanched vegetables and pour the water with one hand into the rava mixture while mixing with a spatula with the other hand.

Mix well. You can see the khichdi thickening while the water starts to bubble around. Simmer the flame now. Close with a lid a let it cook for 4-5 minutes.

Switch off stove and keep the khichdi closed with a lid so that the khichdi gets further cooked in the heat and it will become grainy and separate instead of being mushy.

You can add another tbsp of ghee, roasted cashews and mix well before serving the hot khichdi with coconut chutney and sambar.

Indian-spiced chard with tofu

Ingredients
1 large bunch of red swiss chard or rainbow chard (around 16 to 18 leaves)
3 tablespoons olive oil
1 onion, chopped
1 tablespoon ginger, minced
3 cloves garlic, minced
1 teaspoon turmeric
1 teaspoon garam masala
1/2 teaspoon red chili flakes
1 teaspoon cumin powder
1 teaspoon kosher salt
1 tomato, chopped
1 block extrafirm tofu, cubed
1 cup water
1/4 cup roasted cashews, for garnish
1/4 cup chopped cilantro, for garnish

Directions
Rip leaves of chard of stalks and set stalks aside. Chop chard leaves into bite-size pieces, then wash and drain thoroughly. Rinse stalks, then chop.
Heat the olive oil in a large pan. Add the onions, garlic, and ginger and sauté until golden brown — about 3 minutes. Add the chard stalks. Sauté 1 to 2 minutes more.
Add the turmeric, garam masala, cumin powder, red chili flakes, and salt. Sauté 3 to 5 minutes until fragrant. Add the chopped tomato and cook until tomatoes break down.
Add chard leaves and cook on medium-high just until the leaves wilt, about 3 minutes. Add the tofu and water. Bring to a boil, reduce heat to med-low and simmer 15 minutes till chard cooks down and the flavors meld together.
Sprinkle with cashews and cilantro just before serving.

Vegetable dum biryani

Prep time: 45 mins
Cook time: 45 mins
Total time: 1 hour 30 mins
Serves: 4-5

Ingredients (measuring cup used, 1 cup = 250 ml):
For the rice layer:
1.5 cups basmati rice, 300 grams
3 to 4 green cardamoms (choti elaichi or hari elaichi)
1 inch cinnamon (dalchini)
1 medium size bay leaf (tej patta)
2 star anise (chakriphool)
1 black cardamom (badi elaichi)
5 cups water for cooking rice
¾ tsp salt or add as required
For the veg gravy layer:
2 large onions, finely sliced or 2 cups thinly sliced onions or 200 grams onions, sliced
1 tbsp ginger garlic paste (1 inch ginger + 7 to 8 garlic crushed in mortar-pestle)
2 medium size carrots, chopped
1 medium size potato, chopped
½ cup cauliflower florets/gobi (i did not add cauliflower)
4 to 5 button mushrooms, chopped
¼ cup chopped french beans
½ cup green peas/matar
1 cup fresh yogurt (200 grams) or cashew yogurt, beaten or whisked till smooth
½ cup water for pressure cooking and ¾ cup water if cooking in a pot
½ to 1 tsp red chilli powder (lal mirch powder)

3 to 4 tbsb oil or ghee (i used sunflower oil)
Salt as required
Biryani masala:
1 inch cinnamon stick (dal chini)
4 cloves (laung)
4 green cardamoms (choti elaichi or hari elaichi)
A single blade of of mace/javitri (not the whole mace. mace is a strong spice)
Topping the layers:
¼ cup fried browned onions
A few strands of saffron/kesar dissolved in 2 tbsp warm milk or water.
¼ cup fresh mint leaves, chopped (pudina)
2 tbsp oil or butter or ghee

How to make the recipe:
Prepping rice:
Rinse the rice very well in water till it runs clear of starch. then soak the rice for 30 mins in enough water. after 30 minutes drain the rice.
Heat water first in a deep bottomed pan. add all the whole spices.
Cook the rice till the grains are 75% cooked.
Drain the rice in a colander and keep aside.
Preparing the biryani masala powder:
In a spice grinder or small dry grinder, grind all the spices mentioned for the biryani masala to a powder. keep aside.
Preparing the vegetable gravy:
Heat oil in the pressure cooker or pan.
Add the thinly sliced onions. saute them on a low to medium flame, till they get golden. then remove ¼ cup of the fried onions and keep aside.
Now add the ginger-garlic paste to the ¾ of the browned onions in the cooker or pan.
Stir and saute till the raw aroma of ginger-garlic goes away.

Now add the freshly ground biryani masala & red chilli powder. stir.
Add the mix chopped vegetables and stir for some 3-4 mins on a low flame.
Reduce the flame and add the yogurt slowly, stirring it.
Now add water and salt. stir very well.
Pressure cook the veggies for 1 whistle.
Assembling and layering:
In a small bowl take 2 tbsp milk. add saffron strands and mix well. keep aside for 10 to 15 minutes.
If baking then use a pyrex bowl or deep pan. if cooking on stove than use the same pan in which you cooked the veggies or a different one. you can make as many layers you want.
Arrange half of the veg gravy in the pan or pyrex bowl.
Now spread half of the cooked basmati rice on top of the veg layer.
Sprinkle half of the mint leaves, 1 tbsp oil/ghee and the saffron milk.
Also add half of the fried onion evenly on this layer.
Top this layer with another layer of veg gravy.
Then again the rice layer.
And finally with mint leaves, 1 tbsp oil/ghee, saffron milk and fried onions.
Cover the pyrex bowl with an aluminium foil.
If using a pan, then cover the pan with a moist muslin cloth or aluminum foil. cover tightly with a lid.
You can bake the biryani for 25 to 30 minutes in a preheated oven at 180 degree celsius.
If cooking on stove, then first heat up a tava/griddle and then keep the biryani pan on the tava. this way the bottom of the biryani won't get burnt. lower the flame and let the biryani dum cook for 25-30 minutes or till done.
Serve vegetable biryani hot with some raita, pickle, salad and papad.

Daal: indian spiced lentils

Serves: 4
Total time-50 mins

Ingredients
1 ½ cups red lentils, washed and drained
1 ½ tbsp. ghee ('samna' in arabic)
1 large onion, finely diced (i like to use a food processor)
3 cloves garlic, minced
1 tbsp. grated fresh ginger
2 small red chillies or ½ tsp. dried red chilli flakes (optional)
1 tbsp. curry powder
1 tsp. ground coriander
1 tsp. ground turmeric
½ tsp. ground cumin
½ tsp. ground cinnamon
1 large tomato, finely diced
4-5 cups water
salt & pepper to taste

Instructions
In a large pot over low-medium heat, add the ghee to melt. Add the onion and cook, stirring until very soft and translucent and slightly yellow, about 6-8 minutes.
Add the garlic, ginger and fresh chilli if using (if using dried red chilli flakes, add them later with the spices) and cook for 1 minute, until just fragrant.
Add the spices; curry, coriander, turmeric, cumin, cinnamon and dried red chilli flakes (if using). Stir for about 30 seconds.
Add the tomato and the lentils, stir for a couple of minutes until nicely coated with everything.
Add 4 cups water, bring to a boil and lower the heat to a simmer. Cook, partially covered for about 20-30 minutes until

lentils are very soft and the stew is thick, stirring occasionally to prevent sticking and adding a little extra water if needed. Serve with naan and mango chutney.

Indian-spiced eggplant & cauliflower stew

Ingredients
2 tablespoons curry powder, preferably hot madras (see note)
1 teaspoon garam masala, (see tip)
1 teaspoon mustard seeds
2 tablespoons canola oil
1 large onion, sliced
2 cloves garlic, minced
1 teaspoon finely grated fresh ginger
3/4 teaspoon salt
1 1 pound eggplant, cut into 1-inch chunks
3 cups cauliflower florets
1 15 ounce can diced tomatoes
1 15 ounce can chickpeas, rinsed
1/2 cup water
1/2 cup nonfat plain yogurt, (optional)

Directions
Heat a dutch oven over medium heat. Add curry powder, garam masala and mustard seeds and toast, stirring, until the spicesbegin to darken, about 1 minute. Transfer to a small bowl.
2.
Add oil, onion, garlic, ginger and salt to the pot and cook, stirring, until softened, 3 to 4 minutes. Stir in eggplant, cauliflower, tomatoes, chickpeas, water and the reserved spices. Bring to a simmer. Cover, reduce heat and cook,

stirring occasionally, until the vegetables are tender, 15 to 20 minutes. Top each serving with a dollop of yogurt, if desired.

Dal makhan

Ingredients
3 cups cooked black lentils
1 cup cooked red kidney beans
1 tablespoon vegetable oil
1 red onion
1 tablespoon minced ginger
3 cloves minced garlic
1/2 teaspoon each dried spice: salt, turmeric, corriander, cumin, cayenne
1+ cup tomato puree
1/2 cup raw cashews (or 2/3 cup soymilk)
Cilantro, to garnish
Basmati rice or naan, for serving

Directions
Prep: soak about 1/2 cup raw cashews to make a cashew cream that will add a ton of creaminess to the soup. If this isn't possible, you can sub non-dairy milk.
Step one
First, cook the black lentils and red kidney beans. You can certainly use canned or pre-cooked ones, but the flavors will be so much better if you start with the dry legumes and cook them yourself (especially with the lentils). Either way, prepare these, drain them, and set aside.
Step two
In a deep skillet, warm a tablespoon of vegetable oil and add in a diced red onion, 3 minced cloves of garlic, and 1 tablespoon of minced ginger. Allow these to soften and then add in the spices right onto the onions: start with 1/2

teaspoon each salt, turmeric, corriander, cumin, cayenne. Give these 5 minutes.

Also, now would be a good time to start thinking about the rice (or naan bread) that you'll be serving with this dal...

Step three

Next, add in the lentils, beans, and about a cup of pureed tomatoes. Use a fork to mash the lentils and beans right in the skillet. They don't have to be 100% mashed, just break them up a bit. Then allow this to simmer for at least 25 minutes, stirring regularly and adding water as necessary to maintain the stew-like consistency.

Step four

Meanwhile, make the cashew cream. Simply blend the cashews with about 1/2 cup of water until completely smooth. Add half of this into the dal and reserve the other half for garnish.

Step five

After about 25 minutes of simmering, give this a final taste and feel free to add any additional spices that are needed. Then, divide into bowls, drizzle on some cashew cream, add a garnish of cilantro, and serve with basmati rice or fresh naan

Crispy potato red lentil dal

[makes 5 servings]

Ingredients
¾ pound small yellow potatoes, quartered
2 tablespoons olive oil, divided
2 teaspoons cumin seeds, divided
½ teaspoon fennel seeds
1 red onion, diced
2 cloves garlic, minced
1 inch knob ginger, peeled and minced
1 teaspoon ground coriander
1 teaspoon ground turmeric
1 teaspoon ground cinnamon
1 cup red lentils
1 can (14 ounces) light coconut milk
1 ½ cups low sodium vegetable broth
2 cups baby spinach or kale
salt & pepper to taste

Directions
Preheat oven to 425 degrees f, rack in the middle. Line a baking sheet with parchment paper.
In a large bowl gently toss quartered potatoes, 1 tablespoon olive oil, cumin and fennel seeds, and salt and pepper. Transfer to baking sheet and bake for 25 minutes, or until potatoes are fork tender, crispy, and golden. Set aside.
Meanwhile, in a large dutch oven or heavy pot, heat remaining tablespoon of olive oil over medium heat. Add onion, garlic, and ginger and sauté, stirring frequently, until onion becomes very soft (about 8-10 minutes). Grind the remaining teaspoon of cumin seeds with a mortar and pestle or coffee bean grinder and add with remaining spices,

coriander, turmeric and cinnamon, to the pot. Continue stirring for 1-2 minutes, or until spices are very fragrant. Stir in lentils, coconut milk, vegetable broth, and salt and pepper and bring pot to a boil. Reduce heat to low, cover, and allow to simmer for 25-30 minutes, or until dal appears very creamy. Remove from heat, then stir in the baby greens and crispy potatoes until greens just begin to wilt. Serve and enjoy!

Nutritional information [per serving = 1 cup]
225 calories, 11g fat, 26g carbohydrates, 6g fiber, 3g sugar, 6g protein

Paneer bhurji kati rolls

(makes 8 rolls)

Ingredients
450g paneer, crumbled
50g butter
1 large red onion, diced finely
1 tsp cumin seeds
2 tbsp freshly-grated ginger
2 hot red chillies, chopped finely
½ green pepper, diced finely
handful shredded red cabbage
handful petits pois or peas
3 spring onions, sliced at an angle
½ tsp amchur powder
1 tsp garam masala
½ tsp turmeric powder
1 tsp salt
juice of half a lemon
fresh coriander, to garnish
8 chapattis or paratha
salad leaves, to serve

Method
1. Melt the butter in a large pan and add the cumin seeds. Allow to sizzle a little bit, and then add the chopped red onions and red cabbage. Cook on a medium heat, stirring frequently until soft.
2. Next, add the ginger, chillies, pepper, petits pois, amchur powder, garam masala, turmeric powder and salt. Allow to cook for 5 minutes on a low heat.
3. Finish by adding the paneer and lemon juice. Cook this on a medium heat for around 5 minutes, stirring often. Don't let

this become too dry – you want the paneer to stay juicy for your kati rolls.
4. Garnish with fresh coriander and spring onions.
5. You Can either serve the bhurji like a curry with hot chapattis or naan or you can make perfectly-portable kati rolls.
6. To make kati rolls, take a hot chapatti or paratha and put some filling inside. You can also add some fresh salad and chutney at this stage (i love sriracha and green coriander chutney in these). Roll them up tightly and wrap with greaseproof paper.
Serve hot with cold lassi, beer or a steaming cuppa chai.

Rice and lentil curry bowls with cilantro cashew sauce

Serves: 6

Ingredients
For the cilantro cashew sauce:
½ cup fresh cilantro
¾ cup cashews (mine were salted)
⅓ cup water
¼ teaspoon salt
Juice of 2 limes
1 clove garlic (optional)
1-2 teaspoons honey
For the roasted carrots:
8-10 carrots, peeled and chopped into chunks
1 tablespoon olive oil
1 teaspoon garam masala
½ teaspoon chili powder
Salt to taste
For the rice and lentil curry:
1 cup basmati rice
1 tablespoon oil
½ cup chopped onion
2 cloves garlic
2 tablespoons red thai curry paste
1 teaspoon garam masala
½ teaspoon cumin seed (or ground cumin)
1 cup brown lentils, rinsed
14 ounces tomato puree
2 cups chicken or vegetable broth
Pinch of salt
Avocado and cilantro for topping

Instructions

For the sauce, puree all ingredients in a food processor or blender until smooth. Taste and adjust.

For the carrots, toss all ingredients together. Roast at 450 degrees for 20-30 minutes or until golden brown and roasty. <-- favorite word.

Cook the rice according to package directions. I used a rice cooker.

For the curry, heat the oil in a skillet over medium heat. Add the onion and garlic; saute for 3-5 minutes. Add the curry paste and spices; saute for 2-3 minutes.

Add the lentils, tomato sauce, and broth. Simmer until lots of the liquid has evaporated - continue adding ½ cup of liquid as needed (the lentils will just keep soaking it up). Repeat this process for about 30-45 minutes until the lentils are soft.

Add the rice to the lentil mixture; stir to combine, adding extra broth or water as necessary. Season with salt.

Serve in bowls topped with the roasted carrots, avocado slices, cilantro, and cilantro cashew dressing.

Gobhi matar a homemade preparartion of cauliflower and green peas.

Preparation time : 5-10 minutes
cooking time : 12-15minutes
servings : 4

Ingredients
Cauliflower, separated into florets : 1 medium
green peas, shelled : 1 cup
olive oil : 2 tablespoon
cumin seeds : 1 teaspoon
ginger paste : 1 teaspoon
garlic paste : 1 teaspoon
coriander powder : 2 teaspoon
red chilli powder : 1/2 teaspoon
turmeric powder : 1/2 teaspoon
tomato puree : 1/4 cup
salt : to taste
garam masala : 1 teaspoon
dry mango powder (amchur) : 1/2 teaspoon
green chilli, slit : 1
fresh coriander leaves, chopped : 1 tablespoon

Method
Heat olive oil in a kadai (wok) and add cumin seeds. When they begin to change colour add ginger paste and garlic paste. Sauté for half a minute. Add coriander powder, red chilli powder and turmeric powder. Sauté for another half a minute. Add cauliflower florets, green peas, half a cup of water and tomato puree. Add salt and mix. Cover and cook for eight to ten minutes, stirring occasionally add garam masala powder and amchur and mix. Garnish with green chilli and coriander leaves and serve hot.

Part 2

Introduction

India is a multifaceted cultural country because it has numerous states. Each state has their own originality and each one of them brings one authentic twist in the cuisine of India, if not two! The people here are actually a foodie, they love to eat and their method of cooking is rather different from the rest of the cuisines in the world. Amongst all the dishes, what stands apart is their snack items. The possibilities are immense and there is no boundary to which the authenticity stops!

Each of the snack/appetizer recipes vary from one another, and each of them tastes great. Not only the grownups but also the kids love these snack recipes. The wonderful thing about these items is they can be relished as breakfast, or as an afternoon snack.

People even serve these foods in parties and get-togethers. Most of the recipes in the e-book are quite simple to create. Any beginner-level cook would be able to prepare it barring one or two.

Idli or Cooked Rice

PREP TIME
9 hours
COOK TIME
10 mins
TOTAL TIME
9 hours 10 mins

RECIPE TYPE: breakfast, snacks
SERVES: 3-4

INGREDIENTS
- 1 cup cooked or steamed rice
- ½ cup urad dal or split husked black gram
- 10 tbsp strained urad dal water for grinding
- 1 cup idli rava or cream of rice
- Rock salt as required
- Olive oil for greasing

DIRECTIONS
Soak the urad dal overnight or at least for 4 hours.

Soak the idli rava for about 2 hours.

Drain the dal and make sure to reserve the water.

Drain the idli rava and combine it with the urad daal.

Add the cooked rice to it and throw everything into a grinder.

Add 3-4 tbsp of water and then grind until the mix becomes smooth.

Pour into a bowl and season with salt.

Cover and let it sit for 9 hours.

In a steamer, boil 3 cups of water.

Grease the idli moulds and pour the batter into them.

Place it into the steamer and cover with lid.

Let it steam for 10 minutes and the idli is ready!

Khatta Dhokla Recipe or White Dhokla

PREP TIME
8 hours
COOK TIME
25 mins
TOTAL TIME
8 hours 25 mins

RECIPE TYPE: snacks
SERVES: 3-4

INGREDIENTS
- 1 cup regular rice or idli rava
- ½ cup thick sour yogurt or khatta dahi
- ¼ cup urad dal or spilt and husked black gram
- ½ tsp baking soda
- 1 green chili or hari mirch, chopped
- ½ inch ginger or adrak, chopped
- ½ tsp oil to be added later to the batter
- rock salt as required
- 3 tbsp water for grinding
- ½ to 1 tsp olive oil for greasing the pan

DIRECTIONS

Soak the urad dal and rice into a separate bowl for about 4 hours with water.

Drain them well and then grind together until the mixture becomes smooth.

Add 2-3 tbsp of water to it if needed.

Add the green chili and ginger and grind for 2 minutes more.

Pour the mix into a bowl and add yogurt and salt to it.

Let it sit in a warm place for about 8 hours.

Add the baking soda to it and stir.

Grease a pan and pour the batter.

Boil water into a steamer and place the dhokla into it.

Sprinkle the chili powder, roasted sesame seeds and black pepper on top.

Cover and steam for 20 minutes.

Kala Chana Sundal

PREP TIME
8 hours
COOK TIME
30 mins
TOTAL TIME
8 hours 30 mins

RECIPE TYPE: snacks
SERVES: 2-3

INGREDIENTS
- ½ cup kala chana or black chickpeas
- ¾ tsp urad dal or spilt & skinned black gram
- 3 cups water
- 12 curry leaves or kadi patta
- 2 tbsp grated fresh coconut
- ¾ tsp black mustard seeds
- 1 green chili, chopped
- A pinch of asafoetida or hing
- 1 dry red chili, deseeded
- 1 tbsp coconut oil or peanut oil
- Few drops of lemon juice (optional)

- Rock salt as required

DIRECTIONS

Soak the chickpeas overnight and then cook them into the same water until they are tender.

Add a pinch of salt to it and then keep aside for now.

In a pan heat the oil and fry the urad dal.

Add the mustard seeds to it and brown the daal.

Add the red chilies, hing, curry leaves and toss for a minute.

Add the cooked chickpeas to it and toss for 5 minutes on low flame.

Stir in the coconut and squeeze the lemon juice.

Mix well and serve hot.

Sama ke Chawal ki Idli

PREP TIME
9 hours
COOK TIME
10 mins
TOTAL TIME
9 hours 10 mins

RECIPE TYPE: breakfast, snacks
SERVES: 2-3

INGREDIENTS
- 1 cup sama ke chawal or barnyard millet
- Rock salt as required
- ½ cup sabudana or tapioca pearls
- 2 pinches of baking soda

DIRECTIONS

Combine the sabudana and sama ke chawal in a bowl and soak in water for 3 hours.

Grind with some more water into a smooth paste.

Pour the paste into a bowl and let it sit for 9 hours.

Season the batter with salt and then pour into a greased idli mould.

Pour the batter into idli mould.
Boil water in a steamer and place the idli mould into it.
Steam for 10 minutes and serve with chutney.

Desi Tawa Cheese Biscuits

PREP TIME
40 mins
COOK TIME
15 mins
TOTAL TIME
55 mins

RECIPE TYPE: starter
SERVES: 28 to 30 small biscuits

INGREDIENTS
- 1 cup whole wheat flour
- 8 tbsp milk
- ½ cup all-purpose flour or maida
- ¼ tsp baking soda
- 80 grams plain regular cheese, grated
- 3 tbsp olive oil
- Salt to taste
- 40 grams chilled butter
- ½ tsp black pepper or add as required
- ½ tsp baking powder
- 1 tsp corn starch (optional)
- some whole wheat flour for dusting

DIRECTIONS

Combine the flour with salt, pepper, baking powder and baking soda into a large bowl.

Add the butter to it and combine well.

You would have a crumb-like mix. Add in the cheese and combine.

Pour the milk into it and mix well.

Create dough and plastic wrap it.

Refrigerate it for about 30 minutes and then roll out onto a plain surface.

Cut them into round cookies using a cookie cutter.

Add some olive oil to a flat pan or tawa.

Heat on low flame for about 5 minutes.

Make the cookies into batches and serve in room temperature.

Besan Toast

PREP TIME
10 mins
COOK TIME
15 mins
TOTAL TIME
25 mins

RECIPE TYPE: breakfast, snack
SERVES: 2-3

INGREDIENTS
- 1 cup besan or gram flour
- 2 tbsp finely chopped tomatoes
- 5 slices of bread
- 2 tsp finely chopped coriander leaves or dhania patta
- 2.5 tbsp finely chopped onions
- ¼ tsp red chili powder or lal mirch powder
- A pinch of hing
- ¾ tsp finely chopped ginger or adrak
- 2 green chilies, finely chopped
- 2 tbsp oil for frying or as required
- ⅛ tsp turmeric powder or haldi
- 5 tbsp water
- Salt to taste

DIRECTIONS

Combine the onions with ginger, tomatoes, chilies and coriander leaves into a bowl.

Stir in the flour, turmeric powder, hing, chili powder and salt to it.

Mix well and add the water to it to create the batter.

Make sure to make it smooth unless it would take bad.

Cut the breads into triangles and dip them into the batter.

Fry them golden brown on each side with olive oil in batches.

Serve hot.

Hara Bhara Kabab

PREP TIME
20 mins
COOK TIME
15 mins
TOTAL TIME
25 mins

RECIPE TYPE: appetiser, brunch, snack
SERVES: 4

INGREDIENTS
- 2 and ½ tbsp besan or gram flour
- 2 cups spinach or palak
- ¾ cup peas or matar, fresh or frozen
- 2 potatoes or aloo
- 1 tsp aamchur powder or dry mango powder
- 2 tsp ginger-green chili paste
- 1 tsp chaat masala powder
- Salt as required
- 2 tbsp oil for frying the kababs

DIRECTIONS
Chop the spinach and set aside for now.

In a pan mildly roast the flour.

Boil the potatoes and peas into a pot with water and then drain.

Grate the potatoes and combine them with spinach.

Add the peas and chili paste to it.

Combine the mixture with wooden spoon and stir in the spices.

Add the flour to it and season with salt.

Now create flat patties and fry them golden brown in batches.

Aloo Tikki or Potato Fries

PREP TIME
20 mins
COOK TIME
10 mins
TOTAL TIME
30 mins

RECIPE TYPE: snacks
SERVES: 5 to 6 tikkis

INGREDIENTS
- 3 potatoes, 300 grams
- 2 green chilies, finely chopped
- ½ tsp coriander powder or dhania powder
- ¼ tsp dry ginger powder or ¼ tsp minced ginger
- ¼ tsp chaat masala powder
- 3 tsp chopped coriander leaves or dhania
- ½ tsp cumin powder or jeera
- 2 tbsp corn starch
- 2 tbsp oil for frying the tikkis
- Salt as required

DIRECTIONS

Boil the potatoes with water and drain when the potato is tender.

Grate the potatoes and mash them using hands.

Stir in the spices, corn starch, salt and coriander leaves.

Mix well and make flat patties.

Heat the oil in a pan and fry them golden brown.

Serve hot.

Methi Thepla

PREP TIME
30 mins
COOK TIME
30 mins
TOTAL TIME
1 hour

RECIPE TYPE: snacks
SERVES: 11- 12 theplas

INGREDIENTS
- 1 cup whole wheat flour or atta
- 1 cup chopped fresh fenugreek methi leaves
- 1 tsp red chili powder or lal mirch powder
- 1 cup gram flour or besan
- 1 tsp coriander powder or dhania powder
- 1 tsp cumin powder or whole cumin
- ½ tsp turmeric powder or haldi
- 2 tbsp oil
- 1 tsp green chili-ginger paste or hari mirch-adrak paste
- 2 tbsp water
- Salt as required
- Oil for frying

DIRECTIONS

Combine all the ingredients into a large bowl except the water.

Knead using hands and then add a little water.

Create dough and let it rest for 20 minutes.

Make little balls out of it and then roll them out into thin discs.

Fry them with oil and then serve hot with chutney or any vegetable curry.

Sabudana Chiwda

PREP TIME
5 mins
COOK TIME
10 mins
TOTAL TIME
15 mins

RECIPE TYPE: snacks
SERVES: 2-3

INGREDIENTS
- ½ cup nylon sabudana large pearls
- ¼ cup raisins
- ½ tsp powdered sugar
- ¼ cup cashews
- Salt as required
- ¼ cup peanuts
- ¼ tsp red chili powder, chopped
- Oil for deep frying

DIRECTIONS
Heat the oil in a wok and fry the sabudana by putting them onto a strainer.

Fry them in batches.

Place them onto a paper.

Sprinkle the salt, sugar, red chili on it.

Pour into a jug and shake well so everything gets coated.

Add the dry nuts and fruits to it and store.

Rice Pakora

PREP TIME
5 mins
COOK TIME
20 mins
TOTAL TIME
25 mins

RECIPE TYPE: snacks
SERVES: 2-3

INGREDIENTS
- 1 cup cooked rice
- 5 tbsp gram flour or besan
- 1 onion, finely chopped
- ½ tsp carom seeds or ajwain,
- 1 inch ginger or adrak, finely chopped
- ½ tsp coriander powder or dhania powder
- ½ tsp cumin powder or jeera powder
- 1 green chili, chopped
- 6 tbsp water
- ¼ tsp turmeric powder or haldi
- A pinch of hing
- salt as required
- ¼ cup chopped coriander leaves or dhania patta

- Oil for deep frying

DIRECTIONS

In a bowl mash the rice using a spoon.

Stir in the flour, ginger, onion, green chilies, coriander leaves, spices and salt to it.

Combine well and set aside for 10 minutes.

Add the water and mix.

Heat the oil in a skillet and scoop little batches into the skillet.

Fry the pakoras in batches.

Serve hot with sauce.

Appam Without Yeast

PREP TIME
12 hours
COOK TIME
30 mins
TOTAL TIME
12 hours 30 mins

RECIPE TYPE: breakfast
SERVES: 3-4

INGREDIENTS
- 1 cup regular rice
- 3 tbsp husked urad dal
- 1 cup coconut milk
- 1.25 cups cooked rice
- ½ tsp rock salt
- ¼ tsp methi seeds or fenugreek seeds
- 2 pinches of baking soda
- ½ tbsp sugar
- ⅓ cup coconut water
- coconut oil for smearing the pan

DIRECTIONS

Combine the rice, ural dal and methi seeds into a large bowl.

Soak them for about 6 hours with water.

Drain and then pour the milk into the mixture.

Grind the paste until the texture is smooth.

Pour into a bowl and season with salt and sugar.

Let it sit for 12 hours and then stir in the baking soda to it.

Let it sit again for 20 minutes.

In a pan smear the oil and pour the batter using a ladle.

Spread it evenly into a big circle and make it very thin.

When the edges get slightly darker, take off the heat.

Repeat with the rest of the batter and serve hot with any curry.

Onion Rava Dosa

PREP TIME
25 mins
COOK TIME
20 mins
TOTAL TIME
45 mins

RECIPE TYPE: breakfast
SERVES: 2-3

INGREDIENTS
Main ingredients:
- ½ cup unroasted rava or semolina
- ½ cup rice flour
- 2 tbsp all-purpose flour or maida
- 1 green chili, finely chopped
- 1 onion, finely chopped
- 6 curry leaves or kadi patta, chopped
- ½ inch ginger or adrak, finely chopped
- Buttermilk as required
- 10 black peppercorns – crushed
- 1 tbsp chopped coriander leaves

Salt as required

For tempering
- ½ tsp mustard seeds
- 1 tsp oil
- 1 tsp cumin seeds
- Ghee as required for roasting the dosa

DIRECTIONS

Combine the semolina, rice flour, green chilies, onion, all purpose flour, coriander leaves, black pepper, ginger into a large bowl.

In a pan heat some oil and add the mustard seeds.

Add the cumin seeds with the curry leaves.

Toss for about 2 minutes and take off the heat.

Add into the rice mix and mix well.

Season it with salt and pour the buttermilk to it to make a batter.

Let it sit for 20 minutes.

Heat the ghee into a pan and add the batter using a ladle.

Spread thinly in a round shape and then take off the pan when the base is golden.

Repeat the process with others and serve hot with coconut chutney.

Bread Pakora with Stuffed Potato

PREP TIME
25 mins
COOK TIME
40 mins
TOTAL TIME
1 hour 5 mins

RECIPE TYPE: snacks, breakfast
SERVES: 2-3

INGREDIENTS
For the filling:
- 5 boiled potatoes
- 1 tsp aamchur powder
- 1 green chili, finely chopped
- ½ tsp red chili powder
- 2 tbsp finely chopped cilantro
- ½ cup of mint coriander chutney
- black salt

For the outer crisp coating:
- 6 slices of Brown or White Bread
- 3 cups besan or chick pea flour

- ½ tsp ajwain or carom seeds
- ½ tsp garam masala powder
- Salt to taste
- A pinch of hing
- ½ tsp red chili powder or lal mirch powder
- water
- oil for frying

DIRECTIONS
For the filling,
Start by peeling the potatoes and mash them well.

Stir in the green chilies, coriander leaves, aamchur powder, red chili powder and salt to it.

Mix well and adjust the seasoning.

For the batter,
Combine the besan with red chili powder, hing, ajwain, garam masala and salt.

Pour the water and create a medium-textured batter.

Add just a few drops of oil to it and mix.

In a pan, heat the oil.

Cut the breads into triangles and spread mint chutney on top.

Add 2 tbsp of the potato mix and spread over the chutney.

Add another slice of bread on top and then dip into the batter.

Fry them golden brown. Repeat with the rest of the breads.

Eggless Cucumber Cake or Tavsali

PREP TIME
15 mins
COOK TIME
40 mins
TOTAL TIME
55 mins

RECIPE TYPE: Indian dessert, regional, goan
SERVES: 4-5

INGREDIENTS
- 1.5 cups semolina or sooji
- ¾ cup grated fresh coconut
- 3 tbsp cashews, chopped
- 1.5 cups organic powdered jaggery
- 2 cups grated cucumber
- 5 green cardamoms, grounded
- ¼ tsp cumin powder
- ½ tsp coconut oil for greasing the pan

DIRECTIONS
In a pan roast the semolina until the fragrance gets out.

Rinse the cucumber and take out the juice of it.

Combine the semolina, cucumber with its juice, cashews, grated coconut and jaggery in a bowl.

Sprinkle the cardamom powder and cumin powder.

Create a lump-free batter.

Boil some water in a steamer, and grease a pan with coconut oil.

Pour the batter into the pan and place it onto the steamer.

Steam for about 30 minutes and the cake would be ready.

Serve in room temperature or cold.

Matar Kachori

PREP TIME
30 mins
COOK TIME
30 mins
TOTAL TIME
1 hour

RECIPE TYPE: snacks
SERVES: 2-3

INGREDIENTS
For the pastry:
- 1 cup all-purpose flour or maida
- ¼ cup warm water
- ¼ tsp baking powder
- 1 tbsp oil or ghee
- ¼ tsp salt

For the stuffing:
- 1 cup peas
- 1 tbsp besan or gram flour
- ¼ tsp red chili powder or lal mirch
- ½ tsp fennel powder or saunf pwder
- ½ tsp coriander powder or dhania powder
- ¼ tsp cumin or jeera

- ½ tsp chaat masala
- ¼ tsp turmeric powder or haldi
- ½ tsp green chili-ginger paste
- 2 tsp oil or ghee
- ½ tsp aamchur powder or dry mango powder
- salt as required
- 3 cups oil

DIRECTIONS

Preparing the pastry:
Combine the flour with baking powder and salt into a bowl.

Add 2 tsp of oil and then create crumbly mixture.

Pour in water to it and create a dough. Set aside for now.

Preparing the pea stuffing:
Boil the peas with water and drain.

In a pan heat the oil and add the cumin.

Add the ginger and the green chill. Toss for a minute.

Add the spices and salt to it.

Stir in the flour and toss for 4 minutes.

Preparing the kachoris:
Create little balls from the dough and then roll them into 3 inch round discs.

Place the filling in the middle and then seal the edges by picking them in the middle.

Fry them golden brown in batches.

Serve immediately with chutney.

Brinjal Fries

PREP TIME
20 mins
COOK TIME
10 mins
TOTAL TIME
30 mins

RECIPE TYPE: snacks
SERVES: 2-3

INGREDIENTS
- 2 big Brinjal, cut into thick circles
- 5 tbsp gram flour or besan
- A pinch of paprika
- 2 tbsp rice flour
- 1 tsp onion paste
- 1 tsp ginger paste
- ½ tsp coriander powder or dhania powder
- ½ tsp cumin powder or jeera powder
- 3 tbsp water
- ¼ tsp turmeric powder or haldi
- salt as required
- Oil for deep frying

DIRECTIONS

Combine all the spices into a bowl.

Pour water into it. Stir in the flour and coat well.

Add the brinjal into the bowl and marinade it for 20 minutes.

Heat the oil into a skillet and fry them in batches.

Serve hot with chutney or sauce.

Cauliflower Fries or Gobi Pakora

PREP TIME
20 mins
COOK TIME
10 mins
TOTAL TIME
30 mins

INGREDIENTS
- 1 cauliflower florets
- ¼ cup all-purpose flour
- 3 tbsp gram flour or besan
- ½ tsp onion paste
- ½ tsp ginger paste
- ½ tsp garlic paste
- ½ tsp coriander powder or dhania powder
- ½ tsp cumin powder or jeera powder
- Water as needed
- ¼ tsp turmeric powder or haldi
- salt as required
- Oil for deep frying

DIRECTIONS
Boil the cauliflower in salted water for 10 minutes.

Drain and set aside for now.

In a bowl combine all the ingredients together.

Stir well and add the cauliflower into the bowl.

Let it set for 15 minutes.

Heat the oil in a skillet and fry them golden brown in batches of 3.

Pumpkin Flower Fries

PREP TIME
20 mins
COOK TIME
10 mins
TOTAL TIME
30 mins

RECIPE TYPE: snacks
SERVES: 2-3

INGREDIENTS
- 1 pumpkin, peeled, cut into thick slices
- 6 tbsp gram flour or besan
- ½ tsp onion paste
- ½ tsp ginger paste
- ½ tsp garlic paste
- Water as needed
- 1 tsp all spice
- ¼ tsp turmeric powder or haldi
- salt as required
- Oil for deep frying

DIRECTIONS
Combine all the spices into a bowl except the pumpkin.

Coat the pumpkin into the batter.
Leave it in the fridge for 20 minutes.
Heat the oil into a skillet.
Fry the pumpkin golden into batches of 4.
Serve hot with sauce.

Gobi ke Paratha or Cauliflower Tortillas

PREP TIME
20 mins
COOK TIME
10 mins
TOTAL TIME
30 mins

RECIPE TYPE: snacks
SERVES: 2-3

INGREDIENTS
- 1 cauliflower florets
- 2 onion, diced
- 1 cup all-purpose flour
- 2 tbsp gram flour or besan
- 1 tsp onion paste
- 1 tsp ginger paste
- 1 tsp garlic paste
- ½ tsp coriander powder or dhania powder
- ½ tsp cumin powder or jeera powder
- 1 green chili, chopped
- Water as needed
- ¼ tsp turmeric powder or haldi

- salt as required
- ¼ cup chopped coriander leaves or dhania patta
- Oil for deep frying

DIRECTIONS

Shift the flours with salt into a large bowl.

Add all the spices and pour water enough to make a firm dough.

Let it set for 10 minutes.

In a pan heat some oil and fry the onion.

Add all the pastes and add the cauliflower to it.

Pour some water to steam the cauliflowers.

Season with salt and add the coriander leaves and stir well.

Now make little balls out of the dough.

Roll each ball into thin round disc.

Place the cauliflower filling in the middle and pull the centers in the middle.

Roll the ball again and roll out in round disc again.

Repeat the process with the remaining dough and fry them golden brown with oil.

MAIN DISHES

Braised Okra (Bhindi Masala)

Okra is well cherished among the Northern Indians and is widely available during the hot summer months. If cooked fresh and picked while tender, the dreaded slimy texture of okra can be eliminated. Served as part of the main course, this recipe presents a crispy, spicy and crunchy balance of that lady finger.

Serves 4 persons

Ingredients:

½ olive oil

1 lb okra, stems trimmed and sliced in rounds

2 medium red potatoes, diced

1 medium yellow onion

2 teaspoon chopped fresh garlic

2 Tablespoon chopped fresh ginger

2 teaspoon ground cumin

2 teaspoon ground coriander

¼ teaspoon turmeric

1 tomato, chopped

Salt to taste

½ cup water

Directions:

Heat ¼ cup of olive oil in a large skillet over medium heat. Add okra and potatoes and fry for 1 minute undisturbed. Continue to cook the okra for another 3 to 4 minutes tossing and turning. Remove from the pan and set aside.

Heat remaining ¼ cup of olive oil over medium-high heat. Add onions and cook until translucent, about 3 to 4 minutes. Add ginger and garlic and continue to cook for another 10 minutes until mixture is golden brown, stirring frequently.

Add cumin, coriander, turmeric to the onion mixture and toast the spices for 30 seconds. Add the chopped tomatoes and stir the mixture.

Add okra and potatoes to the onion tomato and spice mixture. Add salt and 1 cup of water. Bring the mixture to boil. Once it reaches the boiling state, reduce the heat to low, cover the okra and continue to cook until okra and potatoes are tender. About 10-15 minutes.

Pairs well with – Naan, plain steamed rice

Coconut Cashew and Golden Raisin Poha

Poha is flattened rice, similar to rolled oats. This brunch dish is popular among the Gujaratis and Marathis of India. Traditionally made with potatoes and peanuts. Instead, cashews and golden raisins are used to provide the crunch and add the sweet and tart balance to the dish. The coconut provides the texture and flavor. This is just one of the ways to make this quick sweet and savory dish. Whichever way you decide to make it, this dish is one of the easiest and fastest to prepare with very satisfying results. This makes for a great breakfast dish or a one pot meal in itself.

Serves 2-4

Ingredients:

3 Tablespoon olive oil

1 teaspoon black mustard seeds

1 large yellow onion, diced

4 cups thick poha

1 teaspoon ground turmeric

1 teaspoon salt or to taste

½ cup coconut, shredded

¼ cup cashews

¼ cup raisins

A big bunch of cilantro, chopped

3 to 4 lemon wedges

Directions:

Place a wide-bottomed skillet on a medium-high heat, roast the cashew for a few minutes until the color changes to a golden brown. Stir frequently. Once roasted set aside. In the same pan, heat the olive oil and add the mustard seeds. Let it heat until it pops. Once the mustard seeds start to pop add onions and caramelize it for 10 minutes.

In the meantime, take the poha and rinse it under cold water for a few minutes, until thoroughly wet. Drain and set aside.

Once the onions are caramelized, add coconut, turmeric and salt. Stir well and cook for a few minutes. Add the drained poha, stir and cover with the lid. Let the poha steam on medium-low heat for 5 minutes. Check the doneness of the poha and if it is sticking on the bottom, add some water, stir and cover for a few more minutes.

The poha should be cooked within the 5 minutes. Take it off the heat, add the roasted cashews, raisins and chopped cilantro. Cover and let it cool for a few minutes.

Serve with chai and squeeze with fresh lemon wedge before serving.

Pairs well with – Masala Chai

Savory Spiced Zucchini Lentil Cake (Handavo)

This recipe comes from the Gujarati region of India. It is commonly served for breakfast with masala chai or as a snack. This is a fermented cake that rises naturally on its own. The cake can also be served as part of a main course with vegetables.

Serves 6 - 8

Ingredients:
For the batter:
1 cup green split peas (Channa Dal)
½ cup white rice
1 cup plain yogurt (tart if possible)
1 lb zucchini, shredded
½ cup green peas, cooked
2-inch knob of fresh ginger, grated
3 garlic cloves, finely chopped
Salt, to taste

For tarka:
2 Tablespoon sesame or olive oil
1 teaspoon mustard seeds
1 teaspoon sesame seeds
3-4 curry leaves

Directions:

The day before cooking clean the split peas. Rinse and drain. Cover with enough water and soak overnight. In another bowl, rinse and drain the rice. Also cover with enough water and soak overnight.

Next day, drain and rinse the lentils and rice. In a food processor, blitz the lentils, with yogurt and rice in batches. Transfer into a bowl, add salt, ginger, garlic, cover and let it ferment in the refrigerator overnight.

Next day, remove the batter from the fridge, let it reach room temperature.

Preheat the oven to 350 F.

Add the zucchini and peas to the batter. Stir to mix well and adjust salt if necessary.

Line an 8" square baking dish with parchment paper with overhang. Transfer the batter into the baking dish.

Prepare the tarka by heating the oil in a shallow skillet. Add mustard seeds, sesame seeds and curry leaves. Once the mustard seeds start to pop, add the tarka on top of the batter in the baking dish.

Slide the baking dish into the oven and bake until golden brown and a knife inserted into the center of the cake comes out clean. This will take about 50 minutes to an hour.

Pairs well with – Masala Chai, Cilantro Chutney, Raita

Khichadi (Lentil Rice Porridge)

One of the most basic Indian comfort foods. Also popular as peasant food, this heart-warming dish is as delicious as a fancy gourmet dish at a five-star restaurant. This makes for a great one-pot meal.

Serves 4 persons

Ingredients:
1 ¼ cup long grained rice such as basmati or Jasmine
½ cup yellow mung dal or red lentils
3 Tablespoon ghee or clarified butter or olive oil
4-inch cinnamon stick
3 cloves
1 teaspoon cumin seeds
1 medium onion, chopped
2 teaspoon garlic, minced
1 tsp ginger, minced
Salt to taste
¾ teaspoon ground turmeric
3 ½ cups water

Directions:
Rince dal and rice and let it soak for 30 minutes to an hour.

Heat the ghee or oil on a wide-bottomed pan and let it heat for a few minutes. Once heated, add the cinnamon stick, cloves and cumin. Stir them for a few minutes.

Add onions and cook until translucent and lightly caramelized, about 8 to 10 minutes.

Add ginger and garlic continue to cook for a few more minutes.

Add salt and turmeric.

Drain rice and lentil mixture and add it to the pan.

Add the water and bring the mixture to boil.

Cover and simmer for about 25 minutes.

Pairs well with – Raita, Cilantro Chutney, Salty Chaas

Baingan Bartha (Spicy Roasted Eggplant)

One of the popular main dishes found at a typical Indian restaurant, this version provides a quick way to breakdown the eggplant into a silky texture while adding a huge flavor with minimal effort.

Serves: 2-4

Ingredients:

2 lbs eggplant

4 Tablespoon olive oil or ghee, divided

Salt

½ cup water

1 large yellow onion, diced

2 ripe tomato, cubed

3 cloves garlic, finely chopped

1 Tablespoon ginger, grated

2 teaspoon garam masala

Directions:

Prepare the eggplant by rinsing them first and slicing into 1-inch rounds. Salt the eggplant rounds and stack them on each other. Let it sit for half an hour to release some of the water. After the half hour is up, pat dry the eggplant.

In a large wide-bottomed skillet heat 2 tablespoons of oil or ghee on a medium-high heat. Add the eggplant and cook until it absorbs the oil or the ghee and becomes translucent. Set aside.

In the same skillet heat the remaining oil on a medium high-heat. Add the onions and cook until golden brown. Add the ginger and garlic and cook for several more minutes.

Add the tomatoes and cook until juices are released. Add the eggplant back to the mixture. Sprinkle the garam masala and a teaspoon of salt. Add water and bring to boil. Cover and simmer on medium heat until the water is absorbed and the eggplant is cooked.

Uncover, let it cool slightly. Taste and tweak the spices and salt. Serve hot.

Pairs well with – Naan, plain steamed rice, Gobi Parathas or Spiced Lentil Cake

Aaloo Palak Saag (Spiced Potatoes with Spinach)

This dish transforms the familiar spinach into something velvety and luxurious without too much effort. Spinach pairs well with the bitterness of fenugreek, spiciness of ginger and starchiness of the potatoes. Relatively easy to prepare, this dish is perfect for weekday meals or a dish to share with friends and family alike. Spinach in this dish can be used fresh or frozen. I prefer the convenience of the frozen spinach.

Serves 6 to 8

Ingredients:

2 lb frozen spinach, thawed
1 lb Yukon gold potatoes (about 4 to 5 medium potatoes)
5 Tbsp ghee or olive oil
1 tsp cumin seeds
1 tsp fenugreek seeds, optional
2 inch knob of fresh ginger, grated
2 green chilies, seeded and minced
½ tsp ground ginger
½ tsp ground fenugreek powder
1 ½ tsp kosher salt, or to taste
½ tsp turmeric
2 cups water
1 Tbsp fresh squeezed lemon juice

Directions:

Prepare the potatoes by rinsing it under cold water. Drain in a colander. Check for any black spots on the potatoes, peel them off. With the remaining peel intact, cut the potatoes into medium-large cubed chunks.

Heat oil in a wide-bottomed skillet, add the cumin seeds and fenugreek seeds. Once the seeds start sizzling, add the potatoes, stir, add a few drops of water and cover with the lid and cook over medium-high heat.

Meanwhile prepare the frozen spinach by thawing it in the microwave.

Check the potatoes, by opening the lid and giving it a few stirs. Add the fresh ginger, chilies.

Add the spinach and its water to the potatoes. Stir. Add the ground spices – ginger, fenugreek, turmeric. Add salt. Add 2 cups of water and stir to mix well.

Cover the lid and cook the spinach potato mixture for 20 minutes.

Uncover the lid, check for the doneness of the potatoes. The potatoes will be close to being cooked. Cook the spinach and potato mixture uncovered for another 20 minutes or so until the water is cooked off.

Remove from heat, cool and add the freshly squeezed lemon juice.

Pairs well with – Naan, biryani or plain steamed rice

Vegetable Biryani

Biryani is a traditional rice dish from the southern state of Andhra Pradesh. It is usually cooked with meat like lamb, goat or chicken. This modified version includes a variety of vegetables to satisfy the taste buds of the vegetarian community. The long and detailed process associated with cooking a traditional biryani makes it a special delicacy suitable for festival season.

Serves 8 to 10

Ingredients:
For the spice blend:
1 Tbsp cumin seeds
2 Tbsp coriander seeds
5 to 6 black peppercorns
8 cloves
2 bay leaves
1 dried red chili
1 tsp cardamom seeds

For the vegetables:
4 Tbsp oil, divided
½ head of cauliflower, cut into florets
Salt, to taste
2 cup French green beans, chopped
3 carrots, cubed
1 cup green peas, parboiled
3 medium, Yukon gold potatoes, cubed
1 small red onion, thinly sliced
2-inch ginger, peeled and grated
6 cloves garlic, crushed
½ cup greek yogurt

For the rice:
3 cups basmati rice
3 bay leaves
4 cardamom pods
1 tsp salt

For the saffron milk:
1 cup whole milk
1 tsp saffron, lightly crushed

For the dough:
¾ cup chapatti flour

¼ cup hot water

1 tsp canola oil

Directions:

1)   Prepare the spice mixture by dry roasting on medium-low heat cumin seeds, peppercorns, coriander seeds, cloves, bay leaves, and red chili and cardamom seeds until fragrant. Remove from heat, use a spice or coffee grinder to blend the spices. Set aside.

2)   Rinse the rice thoroughly. In a bowl, cover the rice with water and let it soak while preparing the spice blend and vegetables.

3)   Make the vegetables – In a medium-sized skillet, heat oil over medium heat. Add cauliflower florets and a generous amount of salt. Continue to cook for about 8 to 10 minutes or until the cauliflower starts to get tender. Remove from the skillet and set aside.

4)   On the same skillet, heat another tablespoon of oil over medium heat. Add chopped beans and salt. Cook for 5 minutes or until halfway cooked. Add carrots and cook for 5 minutes or until cooked through. Add peas, cook for 2 more minutes. Remove from the skillet and set aside.

5)   On the same skillet, heat another tablespoon of oil over medium heat. Add potatoes and salt. Add ¼ cup water, cover and cook for 10 minutes or until starting to get tender. Remove from the skillet.

6)   On the same skillet, heat the remaining oil. Add onion slices and cook for 5-8 minutes or until caramelized.

7)   To the onions, add ginger garlic and cook for 2 minutes. Add back all the vegetables along with yogurt, masala and salt. Cook for 5 to 6 minutes. Set aside.

8)   Preheat the oven to 400 F.

9) Make the rice – drain the soaked rice. In a sauce pot, combine rice, enough water, salt, bay leaves and cardamom pods and bring it to boil. Boil for 10 minutes or until ¾ way cooked or slightly tender. Drain and set aside.

10) Make the saffron milk – in a sauce pan, add milk and bring to a gentle boil. On a low-heat add crushed saffron and stir well for a 30 seconds to a minute. Set aside.

11) Divide the rice in thirds and in one thirds of the rice, stir and fold half of the saffron milk mixture.

12) Assemble the biryani – Brush an ovenproof dish lightly with butter or ghee. Layer with half of the vegetable mixture in the bottom. Top with the saffron-milk infused rice. Repeat with rest of the vegetables and rice. Drizzle the remaining over the layered biryani.

13) Roll out the dough so that it is wide enough to cover the pot and place it over the top of the pot and seal by pressing down on the rim or the edges of the pot.

14) Place the pot in the oven for 30 minutes. Once the dough starts appearing golden brown in color, take the biryani out of the oven and let it cool for 10 minutes.

15) Crack open the biryani and serve with raita.

Pairs well with – Baingan Bartha, Mushroom Tofu Vindaloo or any other vegetable curry

DAL / CURRY

Dal Makhani (Kali Dal or Black Dal)

This dish is the creamier and richer version of the basic yellow dal. There is a toothsome bite to the dal as it uses the whole black lentils, also known as Urad dal. Feel free to substitute regular whole milk instead of the cream.

Serves 4-6

Ingredients:

1 ½ cup Urad dal (black lentils)

6 Tbsp ghee, divided

2 large onions, minced

2-inch knob of ginger, grated

Medium head of garlic (about 10-12 cloves), crushed

1 medium tomato, fresh, diced

1 teaspoon cardamom, ground

½ teaspoon turmeric

Salt to taste

1 cup milk

½ cup cream

2 Tablespoon fresh chopped cilantro

Directions:

1)   The night before you plan to make the dal, rinse urad dal in cold water. Transfer in a bowl, cover with lukewarm water and let it stand for 8-10 hours.

2)   On the day of cooking, rinse the lentils. In a large pan with a heavy-bottom, add the lentils. Cover with cold water, bring

it to boil and continue boiling until the lentils are soft and tender. This process can take anywhere from 40-50 minutes

3) While the lentils are boiling, in a separate frying pan, heat 4 Tbsp of ghee. Once heated, add onions and cook until translucent. Add ginger and garlic and cook for another few minutes. Add the turmeric and cardamom and roast the spices for 2 minutes. Add tomatoes, salt and cook for a few more minutes until tomatoes start releasing juice.

4) Add the onion tomato mixture to the lentils after they appear soft when pressed against a spoon. Add the milk and cream. Bring the mixture to boil

5) Cook the lentils until the sauce appears to be getting thick. This process can take from 1 hour to somewhat longer depending on the heat and the stove.

6) Once cooked, garnish with fresh cilantro and serve

Pairs well with - Naan or biryani.

Basic Buttery Mung Dal (Yellow Dal)

This technique of dal making can be applied to any of the lentils or legumes, though mung dal doesn't require as much pre-soaking and cooking as some of the other lentil variations such as – Channa dal, Toovar dal do. The general rule when cooking dal is to pre-soak starting with water for several and up to 8-10 hours. The split and hulled yellow Mung dal doesn't require as much soaking time. The dal is served as part of the main-course accompanied with some of the vegetable dishes, Naan and rice.

Serves 4-6

Ingredients:
1 cup mung dal (split and hulled)
6 cups water
1 medium yellow onion or large shallot, finely cubed
1 teaspoon cumin seeds
½ teaspoon turmeric
1 teaspoon salt or to taste
4 Tablespoon ghee, butter or oil
6 garlic cloves, smashed

Directions:
Rinse and soak the dal in cold water covered at room temperature for 2 hours.

In a medium pot, add the mung dal, water, salt and turmeric and bring it to boil.

Once the dal reaches the boiling point, lower the heat, cover and cook until soft and tender, up to 45 minutes

In the meantime, prepare the tarka by heating the ghee, butter or oil in a skillet over medium high heat, add the cumin seeds, garlic and cook until fragrant. Add the chopped onion or shallot and cook for another few minutes.

Pour the content of the skillets into the pot with dal and stir.

Remove from the heat. Taste and adjust salt to taste

Pairs well with – Naan, biryani or plain steamed rice

Mushroom Tofu Vindaloo

This recipe appears to be daunting, but don't let that set you back. With some pre-planning and preparation, this dish comes together in less than 30 minutes. If possible, prepare the spices and marinade the day before planning to cook. This will allow enough time for the mushroom and tofu to absorb the spice marinade.

Serves 4

Ingredients:

For the Vindaloo Paste:
8 Kashmiri red chilies, deseeded

1 Tablespoon coriander seeds

1 Tablespoon cumin seeds

1 teaspoon yellow mustard seeds

4 cloves

6 black peppercorns

1 medium yellow onion, quartered

2-inch fresh ginger, slices

6 cloves garlic

1 Tablespoon distilled vinegar

½ teaspoon sugar

1 Tablespoon olive oil

1-2 cups warm water

For the mushroom and tofu:
2 packets of button mushrooms

1 lb packet of Extra Firm tofu

1 tsp turmeric

Salt to taste

Directions:

1) Prepare the mushroom tofu marinade by first rinsing the mushrooms and then slicing them by 1" thickness. Remove the tofu from the packet and cut it into medium sized cubes. Add salt and turmeric, rub and keep aside for at least an hour.

2) Make the vindaloo paste by roasting the spices (coriander seeds, cumin seeds, yellow mustard seeds, cloves, peppercorns) on a skillet over low heat. Stir and toast until fragrant. This will take a few minutes. Once cool, add the toasted spices and Kashmiri chilies into the spice grinder and pulse to a smooth powder. Set aside.

3) In a food processor, combine onion, ginger and garlic. Blitz until smooth and set aside in another bowl.

4) In the same food process, add ground spices and vinegar and blitz into a smooth paste. Set aside for an hour

5) After an hour, add the vinegar spice paste, onion-ginger-garlic paste, sugar to the mushroom and tofu marinade. Cover with cling wrap and let it marinate in the refrigerator overnight or 2-6 hours.

6) When ready to cook, take out the marinated mushrooms and tofu and let it come to room temperature by allowing it to sit for 30 minutes.

7) In a heavy bottom pan, over medium-high heat, heat 1 tablespoon of oil. Add mushroom tofu marinade and cook for 5 minutes, stirring often.

8) Add the warm water and bring it to boil, stirring gently. Reduce the heat to simmer, cover and cook until tender, about 20-30 minutes.

Pairs well with – Naan, plain steamed rice and raita

Chana Masala (Garbanzo Bean Curry)

Chana dal is one of the more popular dishes found at the Indian restaurants. Though this dish makes appearance only on special occasions in a regular Indian household. With a bit of preparation, this dish comes together in no time and can be prepared ahead of time and stored for weekday meals.

Traditionally this dish is made from dried chickpeas, 2 can of 15 ounce chickpea can be substituted for 1 ½ cup dried chickpeas used in this recipe.

Serves 4

Ingredients:

1 ½ cup dried chickpeas

1 tsp baking soda

2 inch piece of fresh ginger, grated or finely chopped

3 cloves garlic, roughly chopped

3 Tbsp olive oil

2 medium onions, sliced

- 1 28-ounce can of plum tomatoes
- 1 Tbsp tomato paste
- 1 tsp ground cumin
- 1 tsp garam masala
- ½ tsp turmeric powder
- 1 ½ tsp salt, or to taste

For garnish:
- Lemon wedges
- Chopped cilantro
- Sliced red onions

Night before, rinse and soak the dried beans in a large pot. Add baking soda and cover with water and soak for 8 to 10 hours or overnight.

The day of – Rinse and drain the beans. In a large soup pot, cover the beans with cold water and bring to boil for 45-50 minutes, until soft, discard any scum.

Make a paste of ginger, garlic and salt.

Heat a wide-bottomed large frying pan with oil. When it's hot, add the onions and cook for 12 to 15 minutes until golden brown. When the onions are caramelized add the ginger, garlic paste and stir to mix. Add the tomatoes to the mixture crushing them with your hand before they hit the pan. Add the tomato paste, stir well and cook for 10 minutes.

Add the spices – garam masala, ground cumin, turmeric and more salt if necessary. Cook for a few minutes. Add the cooked chickpeas to the mixture. Stir to mix and check for consistency. Add ¼ cup of water if necessary. Continue to cook for 10 minutes.

Remove from the heat. Garnish with cilantro.

Pairs well with - naan, steamed rice

FLATBREADS / RICE

Naan (Tandoor Bread)

Tandoor ovens are hard to come by, but this bread can be made easily at home either in the oven or on the stove top. Even though it is a yeasted bread, it comes together fairly quickly once the dough has been given proper care and rest. Left over dough can be refrigerated.

Serves: Makes 12 to 16 naan

Ingredients:
3 cups whole-wheat flour
1 cup all-purpose flour
1 cup whole-milk yogurt
¾ teaspoon active dry yeast
2 teaspoon sugar
2 tsp salt
1 tsp baking powder
¼ cup lukewarm water
¾ cup milk (room temp)
Melted butter or ghee for brushing the pan

Directions:

1) Activate the yeast by combining the yeast and sugar in lukewarm water with milk. Stir and let it sit for 5-10 minutes or until it gets foamy.

2) Combine flours, baking powder, salt in a bowl and make a well in the center.

3) Once the yeast mixture is foamy, add milk and yogurt to it. Stir to combine.

4) Pour the liquid mixture into the flour mixture. Mix the dough with wooden spoon to combine.

5) Knead the dough until smooth.

6) Transfer to a bowl that is lightly oiled. Cover with tea towel or plastic wrap and let it rise until doubled in size. This process can take anywhere from 30 minutes to an hour.

7) When the dough is ready, punch it down and divide into equal sized balls – 10, 12 or 16.

8) Take one piece of ball, roll it between your palms, flatten it by pressing between palms and roll it out to your desired thickness.

9) Heat a cast iron skillet over medium-high heat.

10) Once the pan is hot, brush the side of the pan with butter, place the rolled out dough onto the skillet.

11) Let it cook for 1 minute on one side until the dough puffs and bubbles. Flip and let cook for another minute or two until the dough appears cooked into naan.

Pairs well with – curries and Dal

Tomato Rice

This delicious dish will help solve the dilemma if you ever have more tomatoes in your pantry than you know what to do with. This recipe is more popularly made with already pre-cooked white rice and long-grained basmati rice. However, I like the toothsome bite of brown rice and I cook the rice along with the tomatoes as they simmer.

Serves 6-8

Ingredients:

2 Tbsp olive oil

1 Tbsp Urad dal

1 Tbsp mustard seeds

8-10 Curry leaves

5 large tomatoes, chopped, coarsely

1 large yellow onion, chopped

1 Tbsp cumin powder

1 Tbsp coriander powder

1 ½ tsp turmeric

5 cloves of garlic, grated

1/8 cup ginger, grated

1 cup brown rice

3 cups of water

Salt to taste

Directions:

1) Rinse the rice in several iterations of cold water until the rinsed water runs clear.

2) In a large, wide-bottomed sauce pan heat olive oil. Add mustard seeds. Heat until the mustard seeds pop.

3) Add urad dal and curry leaves. Add onions and cook for 5 minutes or until translucent in color.

4) Add ginger and garlic and cook for a few more minutes.

5) Add tomatoes, cumin powder, coriander powder and turmeric.

6) Add rice, water and salt to taste. Bring the mixture to boil.

7) Cover and simmer the mixture until the tomatoes have turned into a sauce and the rice is cooked to a soft consistency.

Pairs well with – Raita, Katchumbar, Baingan Bartha

Gobi Parathas (Cauliflower Stuffed Parathas)

Gobi parathas are a variation to the traditional plain parathas in northern India. It is commonly used at breakfast, however, it can be a good substitute for bread for any meal during the day. It can also be served as snack with hot tea.

Makes about 15 Parathas

Ingredients:
For the dough:
1 ½ cup whole-wheat flour

1 tsp salt

½ tsp cumin power

4 Tbsp olive oil

1 cup lukewarm water

½ cup white rice flour

For the Cauliflower Stuffing:
1 cup grated cauliflower

2 Tbsp olive oil

½ cup cooked peas

1 medium onion

3 cloves garlic

1 inch fresh ginger

1 tsp cumin seeds

1 tsp cumin powder

½ tsp turmeric

Salt to taste

Directions:

1) Prepare the dough by adding the flour, salt, cumin powder and making a well at the center.

2) Add the oil and rub the flour to distribute the oil.

3) Add water and knead the dough to a smooth round ball. The dough will be sticky and soft to touch. Set aside.

4) Prepare the stuffing – In a food processor mince together onion, garlic, ginger and peas.

5) In a wide skillet heat the oil and add cumin seeds.

6) Once the oil is hot, add the grated cauliflower and cook for a few minutes on a medium heat. Add salt.

7) Stir in the onion-garlic mixture to the cauliflower and cook on a gentle-low flame.

8) Stir occasionally until the water released from the cauliflower is cooked off or evaporated. Alternately, if cauliflower is sticking to the pan before it is cooked, then add ¼ cup water.

9) Make the Parathas – Divide the dough in 15 balls. Have the rice flour handy as you will need it to roll out the parathas.

10) Flatten one of the dough balls into a round disk. Place about 2 Tbsp of the cauliflower stuffing in the center. Seal into a ball by crimping together the edges.

11) Roll the stuffed dough ball into the rice flour and roll out the paratha to a somewhat medium-thin round about 6 -8" in diameter.

12) Heat a skillet with oil. Add the rolled out paratha and cook for a few minutes. Flip the side and cook for another few minutes. Check for doneness and repeat the steps with the remaining dough.

Paris well with - Tomato soup or if having it for breakfast then with masala chai.

SIDES

Raita (Cucumber Yogurt)

A common Indian side-dish. This recipe is quick to prepare and is especially cooling when consumed on a hot summer day alongside Khichadi or any of the vegetable dishes presented here.

Serves 4 - 8

Ingredients:

1 cup Greek yogurt

1 medium English cucumber, grated

1 teaspoon Cumin, ground

¼ teaspoon Black pepper, ground

Salt to taste

3 Tbsp. cilantro, finely chopped

Directions:

In a glass bowl, combine yogurt with cucumber along with its juice and stir.

Add cumin, black pepper, salt. Stir. Taste. Adjust salt content as necessary.

Sprinkle with cilantro.

Pairs well with – Khichadi, Spiced Zucchini Lentil Cake, Vegetable Biryani

Kachumbar

Indians are not as much fans of raw veggies. Instead they prefer their vegetables in a quick pickle style with tomatoes, cucumber and red onions. This is a side accompaniment to the dals, vegetables, naan and rice.

Serves 4-6 generously

Ingredients:

1 ripe tomato

1 medium cucumber

1 small red onion

3 Tbsp juice from fresh lemon

½ tsp salt, or to taste

½ tsp cumin powder

2 Tbsp cilantro finely chopped

Directions:

1) Rinse and chop the tomato into tiny cubes by cutting it lengthwise first and then chopping it crossways into cubes. Put the tomatoes into the serving bowl.

2) Peel the cucumber if the skin is thick. If using English or Persian style cucumber skin, leave the peel. Dice the cucumbers and add it to the serving bowl.

3) Chop the onions in small cubes in the same manner as tomatoes. Add it to the serving bowl along with lemon juice, salt, cumin powder.

4) Stir and adjust lemon juice or salt to taste. Refrigerate for at least an hour before serving.

Pairs well with – Naan, Vegetable Biryani, Vegetable curries

Cilantro Chutney

This fresh and green chutney can be used as a spread for sandwiches or it can be used with any of the traditional snacks like samosas, or chaats. The easy-to-find ingredients used in this chutney makes it an essential component of any north Indian household.

Makes 1 pint jar

Ingredients:

1 bunch fresh cilantro

1-inch ginger, sliced

2 Tbsp peanuts, unsalted and unroasted

3 Tbsp dried shredded or desiccated coconut

2 Tbsp lemon juice

1 tsp salt or to taste

Directions:

1) Rinse cilantro by placing it in a bowl filled with cold water. Move the cilantro around and take it out and drain the water.

2) Roughly chop the cilantro leaves along with the stems leaving out any tough stem ends.

3) Add ginger, peanuts, coconut, lemon juice and salt.

4) Pulse them in the blender until the mixture has a smooth consistency. Add water if necessary.

5) Taste and adjust the balance desired for lemony, salty taste highlighting the cilantro's freshness.

6) Spoon it into a jar and refrigerate.

Pairs well with – Kitchadi, Naan, Vegetable Biryani, Gobi Parathas

SOUPS

Tomato Soup

This soup is wonderful on its own, but even better when served with parathas.

Serves 6-8

Ingredients:

3 lb. fresh tomatoes, chopped
4 Tbsp olive oil
1 medium onion, coarsely chopped
3 cloves garlic, sliced
2-inch ginger, chopped
2 tsp cumin seeds
1 tsp cumin powder
1 ½ tsp coriander powder
Salt to taste
3 cups water

Directions:

1) In a large saucepan, heat the oil on a medium-high heat. Add the cumin seeds. Once the seeds sizzle, add onions and cook for 5-7 minutes until translucent in color.

2) Add garlic and ginger to the onion mixture and saute for another 2 minutes, stirring frequently.

3) Add chopped tomatoes and sprinkle the cumin and coriander powder. Add salt. Cook for about 10-15 minutes stirring occasionally.

4) Add the water and bring it to a boil. Lower the heat and simmer the tomatoes for about an hour.

5) Remove from the heat and let the tomato mixture come to room temperature. Once cooled enough to handle, transfer to a blender and blitz in batches.

6) Bring the soup back to the sauce pan, heat gently. Add spices and water according to your preference.

Pairs well with – Gobi Parathas

DESSERTS

Saffron Shrikand with Cashew, Golden Raisin and Honey

Shrikand is a dessert that is creamy, thick and rich without being too heavy. The traditional version involves making the yogurt and straining it in a cheese cloth in an over-night process to remove excess water or whey from the yogurt. Greek yogurt provides us easy access to such thick yogurt and we can skip the overnight step of straining the yogurt here. Generally sweetened with cane sugar or confectioner's sugar, we are substituting honey as the sweetener.

Serves 4 – 6

Ingredients:

2 cups Greek yogurt

½ tsp ground cardamom

4-6 strands of saffron

3 Tsp chopped toasted cashews

3 Tsp golden raisins

6 Tsp honey

This dessert requires very little work

Directions:

1)   Spoon the yogurt in a bowl. Stir in cardamom, saffron, cashews, raisins and honey.

2) Cover and refrigerate for at least an hour for the flavors to meld together.

Pairs well with – Dessert, enjoy on its own

Date Cashew Fudge (Kaju katli)

One of the classic Indian desserts made out of cashews which are soaked overnight and pulverized into a butter. Cashew butter is a good substitute if readily available. This recipe substitutes dates instead of the refined sugar. The use of dates brings out the brown hue to the fudge squares unlike the traditional Kaju katli found in a beige color.

Serves 8-10

Ingredients:

1 cup cashew butter

1 cup dates, pitted and chopped coarsely

¼ cup milk

4 Tbsp ghee

Directions:

1)   Butter an 8-inch square baking dish. Cut parchment lengthwise leaving enough room for overhang and line the baking dish with it and brush it lightly with ghee or butter.

2)   In a medium sauce pan combine dates and milk. Bring it to a gentle boil over medium heat. Simmer the dates in the milk sauce until it turns into a thick paste like consistency. About 10-15 minutes.

3)   Fold in the cashew butter with the milk and date paste. Continue to cook for a few minutes on a low flame.

4)   Remove from the heat and continue to stir to cool slightly.

5)   Pour the mixture into the prepared baking dish.

6)   Smooth out the top with an offset spatula.

7)   Place it in the fridge for 8-10 hours.

8) When ready to serve, cut into squares and serve.

Pairs well with – Dessert, enjoy on its own

BEVERAGES

Fig Milk (Anjeer Doodh)

This is a no fuss preparation dish that is ideal for breakfast or as a dessert. The key is to let the fig infused milk refrigerate for at least 2 hours before being consumed. Ideally whole milk should be used, but a 2% milk would be just fine.

Serves 4

Ingredients:
2 cups milk
2 dried figs, roughly chopped
2 teaspoon toasted chopped almonds

Directions:
In a heavy bottomed pan add chopped figs and milk.

Gently warm the milk with figs until it steams and turn off the heat before it boils.

Let it stand for a few minutes.

Take a spoon, mash figs in warm milk until you see the figs release the seeds and milk changes color to slightly golden.

Gently heat the mixture for a few minutes. Take off the heat and let it cool to room temperature.

Transfer the fig milk into a glass jar or a bowl. Cover and refrigerate it until cold.

Sprinkle with chopped almonds before serving.

Pairs well with – Perfectly delicious on its own.

Masala Chai

A great alternative to coffee in the morning for breakfast. This creamy drink takes after the English breakfast tea except with some spices added. There are many variations to this recipe, and it can be easily tweaked with the spices of your liking such as cinnamon, black pepper and cloves. Whatever spices you choose, start with a small quantity and build up the flavors. Here is the masala tea with tried and tested spice combinations.

Serves 2

Ingredients:

½ cup water

¼ tsp ground cardamom

1 inch round knob of fresh ginger, grated

4-5 fresh mint leaves, gently teared

½ cup milk

1 tsp loose black tea

1 ½ teaspoon honey or to taste

Directions:

In a medium-small sauce pan, add water, cardamom, ginger, mint leaves. Bring to boil

Reduce the heat to medium, add milk and tea. Raise the heat and bring to a rolling boil.

Remove from the heat.

Stir in the amount of honey desired and serve.

Pairs well with - Wonderful on its own for breakfast but also goes well with Gobi Parathas, Spicy lentil cake or Cashew Raisin Poha.

Fresh Honey Ginger Lemonade

Ginger is a cherished ingredient in Indian cooking. Here its spiciness cuts into the sweetness of honey and balances out with the refreshing tartness of the lemon. Served with sparkling water, this beverage is set to win your heart.

Serves 4

Ingredients:
2 Tablespoon ginger, freshly grated
8 Tablespoons lemon juice from freshly squeezed lemons
4 Tablespoons of honey
½ cup water
Sparkling Water

Directions:
Start with combining the freshly grated ginger with the lemon juice in a deep container.

In a medium-small sauce combine water and honey on a low heat and bring to a gentle boil. Remove from heat. Cool slightly.

Pour the honey water mixture over the ginger lemon juice mixture.

Stir to mix well. Refrigerate and serve cold.

Taste the mixture, add cold fizzy sparkling water to dilute the honey ginger and lemon concentrate.

Pairs well with - Enjoy on its own anytime of the day or at the end of a meal.

Salty Chaas

Chaas is traditionally made with buttermilk leftover from churning the fresh butter. The recipe here uses Greek yogurt instead. Enjoy this on a hot day or pour some over the Khichadi or Vindaloo to balance out the heat from the spices.

Serves: 2-4

Ingredients:

1 ½ cup Greek yogurt

1 cup water

1 teaspoon cumin powder

Salt, to taste

2 Tablespoon fresh chopped cilantro

Directions:

In a deep glass container combine the yogurt water and salt.

Use a whisk to briskly stir the yogurt water to combine well. Alternately a blender can be used to blitz the mixture until frothy.

Sprinkle with cumin powder and garnish with fresh chopped cilantro

Pairs well with – Khichadi, Gobi Parathas, Cashew Raisin Poha or as a refreshing cold beverage on its own

Mango Lassi

This sweet and fruity variation of traditional sweet lassi is loved by everyone all over the world. It goes very well with spicy Indian food and helps to cool down.

Serves 4

Ingredients:

1 cup mango Puree from 4 ripe mangoes

1 cup yogurt

½ cup milk

Directions:

1) Place the mango puree, yogurt, milk in a food processor or blender and blitz until combined.

2) If the consistency of lassi is too thick, adjust by adding milk or water.

Pairs well with – Dessert, enjoy on its own

www.ingramcontent.com/pod-product-compliance
Lightning Source LLC
Chambersburg PA
CBHW071830080526
44589CB00012B/974